ACHIEVE
YOUR
BUSINESS
VISION

The essential guide for
ambitious entrepreneurs

ALAN DAVIDSON FCA

R∃THINK PRESS

First published in Great Britain 2019
by Rethink Press (www.rethinkpress.com)

Cover image © iStock / 29mokara

Praise

'Wow, what a great book: really practical, really easy to read and really useful.'
— **Steve Pipe FCA**
Business Author and Former UK Entrepreneur Of The Year

'A staggering 56% of new businesses fail in the first five years, not because the idea was bad but because business has many other facets. This superbly written book is composed from wisdom in business and knowledge of numbers, and is portrayed with passion. It gives an entrepreneur everything they need to know to give their business the best chance to thrive and not just hope to survive.'
— **Shane Lukas**
Author of *What's Next for Accountants* and *Better Business, Better Life, Better World*, Owner of AVN – Inspiring Accountants

Contents

Introduction

I have an unshakeable belief that the entrepreneurs of the world can change things for the better. Most innovation arises either directly from an entrepreneur or because an entrepreneur has forced another organisation to change. This book seeks to give entrepreneurs a head start and a chance to put their ideas into practice much more quickly and successfully than they can at the moment.

I am a chartered accountant who has been advising businesses on financial matters for over twenty-five years. I have seen many would-be entrepreneurs struggle to fulfil their initial expectations, and I have helped them along the way. Often, I could have helped them improve much quicker had I met them much earlier. One way I can help many more people is to encapsulate my thoughts into a book, and here it is.

Achieve Your Business Vision brings together my years of experience (both highs and lows) of working with entrepreneurs, to give you a shortcut to success – so you can transform your business dream into reality and make your contribution to society.

Why do I help entrepreneurs?

I grew up in tough economic times, in the late seventies and early eighties, in a relatively depressed area of the United Kingdom (Wallsend, Tyne and Wear). (Note: there are much worse areas of the world!) I lived on the banks of the Tyne, literally in the shadows of the nationalised shipyard. Every year or so, a royal visitor would make a fleeting visit to launch a huge ship. The whole area worked directly or indirectly for what was then British Shipbuilders, a nationalised industry. Up until around 1973/74, when I was eight years old, it all went reasonably well.

Then the world changed: the huge industries weren't agile and couldn't compete with the new industrialised countries in the Far East. Nationalised shipyards were uncompetitive and lost business. On the surface, lost orders and reduced demand was probably all most people knew.

While the closure of these industries was headline news, the real-life stories that happened as a consequence did not make the press.

The workforce at the time was 100% men – men who had been brought up in a macho world and were the leaders of the household. Consider what happened when the workforce was reduced from 20,000 to 10,000. Overnight!

On a human scale, many, many people were robbed of their self-respect. Many were driven to alcohol. Wallsend had an abundance of watering holes, and it was much easier to spend your days in a drunken state than do something about the social problems. Remember that at that time, 'entrepreneurship' wasn't part of the vocabulary.

Mass unemployment led to riots in some areas (within half a mile of my secondary school, for example). They became no-go areas. Life was quite tough.

When I was twelve, I had my ten minutes with the school careers adviser. I told him I wanted to go to university and qualify as an engineer. He looked at me with disdain and told me to be more realistic – people from my school and background didn't go to university.

Shortly after that, I was cycling through one of the no-go areas on my way home from school. The area had been built in the early sixties and was based on ambitious urban planning ideas. The fourteen-storey blocks of apartments were known colloquially as the 'fourteeners'. They generally stank of urine or antiseptic, depending on whether the local council cleaners had been around recently.

While cycling through this area, I had an experience which fundamentally changed my views on life. I witnessed a person who had lost everything jump from one of the fourteeners. I knew there had been other occasions when this had happened, but I hadn't yet seen it for myself. To this day, some thirty years later, I can still picture the scene.

I determined there and then that my why was to help people transform their lives – to give them a purpose to prevent them from finding themselves in that situation. Although at the time, I didn't realise this had become my WHY. I have since reflected on things and worked through several exercises to delve into what drives me, and it always comes back to that point.

This book is part of that why. The desire to help people transform their lives gives me the motivation to sit down and put pen to paper (or at least to dictate to a computer).

ONE

Shortcut To Success

The best way to learn is to try something and see if it works. If it doesn't, see the experience as a lesson. It's how children learn; it's how society learns. In this book I have pulled together many of the successes and failures I have encountered over the last twenty-five years, both through my clients and in my own business, to help you.

By considering my experiences along with the latest technological ideas, you can avoid the same mistakes and allow your business to take a shortcut to success. It's a fast-moving world, and a six-month setback potentially has a much greater impact now than it would have had twenty-five years ago.

Being an entrepreneur is tough and isn't for everyone. However, for the successful ones it can be both rewarding and great fun. Before you go any further, you need to consider you own situation.

Where do you start?

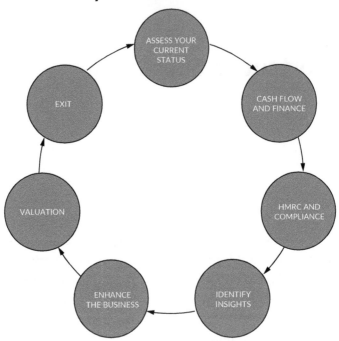

I have put together a structure for success that sets out the ideal steps for launching and growing your business. The steps are outlined above, and the rest of the book delves into each one in more detail. In a perfect world everything would be linear: you would just follow the steps and your business would flourish. In the real world things are a bit different. I advise you to adhere to the structure I've outlined as much as possible, and repeat it whenever necessary, but priorities change, and you will need to adapt as time goes on. Quite often entrepreneurs tell me the whole business thing would be easy if customers, suppliers, team members and the tax inspector weren't there to slow things down!

Assess your situation

Before you can start you need to answer the following questions:

1. What's your business vision and is it on track? Is it congruent with your personal goals?

2. Will your business produce value for its customers?

3. Are there any strategic changes you need to make?

4. Is your business structure appropriate to fulfil your vision?

5. Are you the right person/team to do this?

6. Is the idea feasible?

7. What is the likely funding requirement?

8. How much is the business worth now? How much would you like it to be in your future business vision?

Next, it's time to think about money.

Consider cash flow

A lack of cash can really hamper business growth. You need to consider two separate aspects:

1. Funding (longer-term cash requirements)

2. Day-to-day cash flow

I have seen many businesses attempt to soldier on without addressing the above, and things usually don't end well for them.

Then it's time to move on to the next most-ignored issue.

Follow the rules (HMRC and compliance)

Taxes are a necessary aspect of business, and however unjust you may consider them, you need to make sure all the necessary forms are completed correctly (to your advantage when possible). Where government offers help, make sure you take it. You need to learn about the following:

1. Business taxes

2. Statutory accounts

3. Statutory returns

4. Payroll taxes and returns

5. Value-added tax

6. Capital gains tax

7. Research and development tax credits

8. Inheritance tax

It's easy to concentrate on your customers and improving the business and ignore the boring and sometimes scary stuff. Unless you're an accountant, I recommend outsourcing as much of the above as possible.

Now it's time to start monitoring how it's all coming together.

Identify insights

Insights allow you to make decisions, spot trends, identify problems and fill gaps. In general, they give you the information necessary to take the business to the next level.

Enhance the business

Once you have the insights you can enhance the business. How you do so is highly dependent on the business in question, but it could involve your people, marketing, product development or service delivery, to name a few things.

And while going through all the steps, you need to think of building value.

Build value

In the majority of businesses, value is a function of perceived future profitability multiplied by a multiple. Most people spend lots of time on profitability and not enough on the mysterious multiple.

The best results come from looking at a ninety-day horizon, so work through the steps from the beginning at least every ninety days.

Create an exit plan

When it's time to exit, you need a plan. Although you can sell at any time, without some planning and thought, you'll probably leave a lot of value behind. In many cases, an entrepreneur's business is their most valuable asset, but few know how much it's worth or how to sell it.

The rest of this book goes through the steps in more detail to help you take shortcuts on your way to success and avoid the pitfalls that have caused many before you to stumble.

TWO

Assess Your Situation

At this stage, you need to stand back and take stock of where you are and where you're going. It's so easy to forget to do this. I've seen it happen many times. The entrepreneur and their team focus on the day-to-day problems and opportunities that arise and don't consider the important questions. The key questions to consider are as follows:

1. What's your business vision and is it on track? Is it congruent with your personal goals?

2. Will your business produce value for its customers?

3. Are there any strategic changes you need to make?

4. Is your business structure appropriate to fulfil your vision?

5. Are you the right person/team to do this?

6. Is the idea feasible?

7. What is the likely funding requirement?

8. How much is the business worth now? How much would you like it to be worth in your future business vision?

You have a dream

I often ask clients, 'Why do you do what you do?' And often, the initial answer is 'to make money'. Making money is *never* the ultimate answer. In the end, what the money will give you is the answer. Money drives the ability to fulfil desired experiences and feelings. All our future goals, needs and wants are about having good experiences and feelings.

The other answers usually hinge around time and freedom. It's no good having all the money in the world if you don't have time or freedom to enjoy it.

An entrepreneur can have a great life, with enough time, funds and freedom to enjoy it, if they put the correct foundation in place and build their business on it.

The next question I tend to ask clients is 'What makes your experiences and feelings work for you?'

Simon Sinek explains this well in his TED talk about the power of why. Why do you do what you do? It sounds like a simple question, but you actually need to ask it several times to really understand your why.

It could be to give your family a comfortable existence; it could be to fulfil a childhood dream. But what it's not is to amass money. Look at Bill Gates (Microsoft) – he has a personal fortune so large that most people can't even picture it. He now spends much of his time trying to help rid the world of disease.

In my experience, businesses that know their why are much more successful. If you know why you want what you want, you are much more enthusiastic about and emotionally involved in what you're doing. Business means more than just turning up every day. Drive and nurture your business with purpose.

Once you know your why, you will be able to make decisions with clarity and allow others to support you. It provides motivation in troubled times. So, what is your why? Ask yourself why you do what you do, and you will undoubtedly surprise yourself.

Here's another way to think of it – imagine the epitaph at your funeral. I remember some time ago listening to a business adviser from the US called Michael Gerber. He described the scene: Imagine it's your funeral and one of your loved ones is recounting your life, looking back on what you've done. What would you want this person to say about you?

If they can't say it now, you need to do something about it. You need to act now to put yourself on track to create the life you want described at your funeral. We will all run out of time. We have only one life. The purpose of this book is to help you make the most of the incredible opportunities you have.

Know thy partners

As well as knowing your own why, you should ensure your why is congruent with your business partners'.

A few years ago, I was working with a car-repair business run by a husband and wife team. They employed several mechanics. We went through the exercise of imagining their respective epitaphs. It was plain that the business partners' ambitions differed greatly. The husband wanted to fix cars all day long, while the wife wanted to build and grow a business.

They had been working together for several years prior to our meeting but hadn't ever discussed this or thought it through. Within a month they had gone their separate ways! Some would see this as a disaster, but it gave them both the chance to move on and enjoy their futures.

It's easy to put things off until some distant future point, but doing so usually means they will never get done.

How long do we have?

Use the calculator in the table to work out how long you actually have to achieve your vision.

How long you have to make your mark

	Example	Your numbers
Age you want to exit this business (A)	40	
Age today (B)	30	
Years to make vision a reality (A–B)	10	
How many weekdays per year (W)	260	
How many holiday days per year (H)	35	
How many non-productive days per year (NP)	20	
Average productive days per year (W-H-NP)	205	
Total days to achieve success	(10×205) =2050	

Whatever your number, that's it. This is your time. Now that you know how much time you have to achieve your dream, let's look at what you have going for you.

If you're reading this book, you're fortunate to have been born in a time when opportunity is everywhere. If you had been born in the eighteenth century, you likely would have been a virtual slave to an industrial giant. If you had been born in the fifteenth century, you likely would have been a farmer without many choices in life. Your life would also have been much shorter, and you probably would have died of the plague or some other disease.

Today, with the power of technology, the advances the human race has made, and the sheer diversity that abounds throughout the globe, we have more choice and opportunity than ever before.

Social media gives you the ability to find niche markets across the world. As little as twenty years ago, Yellow Pages was the way to advertise. Teenagers of today (adults of the future) are permanently connected. Your product or service will solve someone's problem, and you can now harness the power of the internet to find many people with that problem, far more than was possible just twenty years ago.

The economy is also much more versatile than ever before. Society now looks up to entrepreneurs. TV shows such as *The Apprentice* and *Dragons' Den* have changed popular culture, and the prevailing climate of aspiration and economic flexibility has made it much easier to set up a business.

In the UK, you can quickly and easily create a business entity from which to develop your idea – sometimes too easily. Indeed, I have seen many individuals create many problems for themselves because setting up a business is so easy. It's also easy to create a mess without correct guidance from the outset, which is why I've written this book. To my mind, wasting your opportunity is not an option.

Translate your personal why to your business

Once you have an idea of your personal why, you need to ensure that it's congruent with your business why. The business why is often called a mission statement. That term is often associated with unreal corporate objectives, so I suggest using the term business why.

Your business why should be to create value for your customers in a way that is congruent with your personal why. For example, my goal is to help transform people's lives, create opportunities for hope, and motivate people. I do these things through the vehicle of my business, which helps my customers (entrepreneurs) do that. In a sense, I'm one step removed from the end goal. I help more people by helping people to help themselves.

To quote a Chinese proverb, 'If you give a man a fish, you feed him for a day – if you teach him to fish, you feed him for many days.'

Why does your business exist?

Your business is a collection of people who've come together in a common goal: to do something, change something or improve something, generally for profit (but not always – your business could exist for charitable purposes).

Your business should always exist to create value for somebody else (your customer), otherwise it's pointless, as nobody would have any need to use your product or service.

You need to determine what you're passionate about, as that passion will be necessary to make your business work. Take a blank piece of paper and a pen and delve into your own experiences and feelings; work out what you really want to do.

As a result, you should be able to fill in the following with your own words:

'To_____ (your contribution) so that_____ (your impact).'

Here are a few examples of company why statements:

- Uber: 'to bring transportation — for everyone, everywhere...'

- Twitter: 'To give everyone the power to create and share ideas and information instantly, without barriers'

- Nike: 'Bring inspiration and innovation to every athlete* in the world. *If you have a body you are an athlete'

Once you have your business why, you can build teams and economics around it. Rooting your business why in your personal why will produce results. Your business why needs to be defined on Day 1, so if you haven't done it yet, then today is Day 1.

Alongside your business why, you should also work out individual value propositions for each service or product that you sell.

The three-step method to simplify this is:

1. Identify your customer's problem, digging deep and extracting as many related problems as you can, to complete the picture for your customer. Most initial problems have many sub-problems related to the headline problem. Ask yourself what the consequence of the problem is. The best way to do this is to ask your prospects/ customers – you need their take on the problem. Ask questions like 'What keeps you awake at night?', 'If you had a magic wand, what would you do to transform your business?' When you receive the answers, delve deeper, to find out

what the consequences of these problems are. This point is so often ignored, but if you don't know the full extent of the problems you can't solve all the problems or assess the true value of what your solution is worth.

2. Having identified your customer's problems, you can now identify the problem-solving benefits of your product or service. You can also ensure you have solved all the problems.

3. You can then assign a value to solving the problems and decide what would be an appropriate value-based price from the customer's perspective. The more unique your solution, the higher the value.

The critical factor in all the above is that you offer relevant products and services that solve problems for your customers in a way that is as different as possible from any potential competitors.

Wherever you are in your business, today is the beginning of the rest of your life. You can change nothing about the past, but you can change everything about your future.

Consider the following analogy. You want to get to Edinburgh, Scotland. The minute you have an endpoint in mind, you can formulate a decision-making process to help you get there. With the endpoint determined, you then need to look around and work out where you are. If your starting point is Auckland, New Zealand, you will need to make completely different decisions than if your starting point is London, UK. In business, working out where you are involves analysis of your current situation.

What is your vision?

Wikipedia defines a vision statement as follows:

> 'A vision statement is a company's road map, indicating both what the company wants to become and guiding transformational initiatives by setting a defined direction for the company's growth.'

Before creating your vision statement, think about this quote from Michelangelo:

> 'The greatest danger for most of us is not that our aim is too high and we miss it, but that it is too low and we reach it.'

Few successful businesses can run without vision – and without a why. How will you know what decisions to make for your business if the vision isn't clear? It's a bit like expecting to successfully cross the Sahara desert blindfolded. Realistically, what chance would you have?

The leader/founder of the business defines the vision. Clearly defining this vision is one of the most important tasks to be carried out in the early stages of the business' life cycle. Your vision should clearly align with your business why.

Is the business why sustainable?

Before you start to develop your business, you need to know if you can make it work from a financial point of view. You may have the noblest business why in the world, but it still needs to work within the constraints of your economic limits. Will it create value for others? Will it be sustainable? Will it fulfil your lifestyle needs?

According to the Office for National Statistics (November 2017), only 44.1% of businesses that started in 2011 survived five years.[1] A staggering 146,130 businesses created in 2011 didn't make it to five years old! And you probably want to do more than just survive.

Remember, today is always Day 1. Whether you're about to start or have already put your ideas into action, do a reality check.

You need to develop a financial plan to make sure your idea is credible. Consider the following:

---

1   www.ons.gov.uk/businessindustryandtrade/business/
     activitysizeandlocation/datasets/businessdemographyreferencetable

- Will the business create value for people? (this is the big one)

- Are there enough potential customers?

- Can you monetise the value into a price?

- What are the costs of production or servicing your customers?

- How many units can you sell now? What is the forecast for the future?

- What are your team costs likely to be? Could you outsource? How much is that likely to be?

- What are the unit costs likely to be, including delivery to the customer?

- Do you need an office/factory? What are the overheads?

- What are the likely personal returns?

- What taxes will need to be paid?

The above list is the bare minimum you need to consider when determining if your idea has a future. It could also be used to predict your financial requirements (which will be discussed in more detail in the next chapter).

FEASIBILITY CALCULATION

Recently, my team were asked to help a start-up restaurant. It was to be a fast-food outlet and was part of a franchise. The entrepreneur was full of enthusiasm and had a business mentor who was encouraging him along. The combination of youth, enthusiasm and some grey hair can be powerful.

I put together a forecast before the project started, and it showed that the business would need to be operated at full capacity for every hour it was open. Clearly this was going to be a challenge. Unfortunately, our entrepreneur was so keen on the idea that he went ahead and invested his life savings in the project.

The landlord granted him a rent-free period, ostensibly to help the business in its infancy. That probably made matters worse, as the reality of the situation didn't hit home for the entrepreneur until he had to start paying full rent. After twelve months, the doors closed. Our client lost the six-figure capital sum he'd put into the business.

Always do a feasibility study, a broad overview. If it indicates the idea won't work in its present form, take action.

Do you have what it takes?

Driving an entrepreneurial business requires vast reserves of personal strength and inner belief. You may have these things, but do you also have the right personality to complement your entrepreneurial drive?

A simple way to determine this is by using the DISC model (formulated by William Moulton), which quickly assesses an individual in terms of four main behaviours: dominance, inspiration, supportiveness and cautiousness.

Most people display a combination of all four with a bias toward one or two of the behaviours, which are briefly summarised below.

A summary of DISC behaviours

Behaviour	Dominant	Inspiring	Supportive	Cautious
Summary	Outgoing and task-orientated	Outgoing and people-orientated	Reserved and people-orientated	Reserved and task-orientated
Typical behaviours	Direct Demanding Decisive Determined Doer	Influencing Impressionable Interactive Impressive Involved	Stable Steady Sweet Status quo Shy	Calculating Competent Conscientious Contemplative Careful

A successful entrepreneur will generally have more D and I traits, and a strong team will possess a combination of all the traits.

How can you benefit from this behaviour analysis? A great team will have a mix of the above qualities, so that they can complement one another. This analysis will also help you to identify potential team conflicts at an early stage.

You should also analyse the personal goals of the management team. By definition, personal goals are individual. If several entrepreneurs are involved in the business, it's critical that personal goals don't conflict. Ideally, all the entrepreneurs' personal goals will align with one another and with the business goals. If one person's goal is to build a business and sell after five years and another wants to create a lifestyle business that provides income for the next twenty years, there could be problems ahead. However, sharing goals at an early stage will allow you to determine this and potentially build the business goals around the management team's personal goals.

Set the business goals

Ignore goal setting and you will achieve less than you could. Goals give you focus and guide your actions.

Let's assume you have the skills and the finances to be successful but no effective goals. What will happen? You will most likely create a business that is random and unproductive.

Along with the skills and finances, you need goals and belief. Goals and belief keep you on track and give you the power to succeed.

THE POWER OF GOALS AND BELIEF

I had a business client that for many years had been manufacturing components. Their customers were large traditional manufacturers, and their goal was to make as much profit as possible. When I first met them, they were making £30,000 net profit a year. I did a 'what if' profit driver analysis, by projecting forward some key changes that the business could make. This showed them that they had the potential to make ten times that. The following year, that's exactly what happened: £300,000 from £30,000. Why?

The key to the change was twofold. Ultimately, the client had gained a clear goal *and* a belief it could be done. I had shown them that by making certain changes, which were all easily achievable, a radical change in profitability was possible.

How can we create goals that work?

You may be familiar with the SMART goal concept. Indeed, SMART goals get the thumbs-up in several research studies.

S – must be specific

M – must be measurable

A – must be attainable

R – must be relevant to you

T – must be time bound

However, research strongly suggests that an attainable goal creates a sense of comfort and therefore doesn't stretch performance. Consider Jack Welch, the CEO of General Electric for twenty years. He pushed for stretch goals, not attainable goals. And in his twenty years as CEO, he increased the company's market value from $12 billion to $280 billion. Discomfort is therefore also an important consideration when it comes to goals.

A paper about GE's stretch goals stated the following: 'If the right environment was created for the group, setting stretch goals and working toward what might seem to be impossible results often became reality.' It gave the example of the train journey from Tokyo to Osaka, which used to take more than six hours. If the Japanese railway executives had said to their engineers 'I want you to reduce the time to six hours,' the engineers would instinctively have thought in terms of small improvements, perhaps in boarding passengers and unloading baggage. But instead the Japanese executives set out a challenge to reduce the time of the journey to three and a half hours. Faced with such an 'impossible' goal, the engineers and designers were forced to re-examine the most fundamental assumptions governing rail travel in Japan. The result of the re-examination was the bullet train.

It is my view that a combination of stretch and attainable goals will create the most successful outcome.

In the case study above, the client set a huge stretch goal: £300,000 profit. Doing so changed their mindset and, as a result, the way they drove things forward. They integrated this mindset with a number of attainable process goals.

Set huge stretch goals to create the big picture, and set achievable process goals that move you toward the big picture. Success will follow.

Structure of the business

Once you've worked out what you want to do and what your goals are, you need to determine how to structure your business. If you're already in business, like many entrepreneurs, the structure you have now may not be the most appropriate going forward. Apathy about the structure can prove costly.

First, you need to decide what legal form the business will take. A century ago this was quite straightforward, but changes in commercial legislation have resulted in many more options. How do you decide? Some factors that you need to consider are privacy, risk management, taxation, ability to raise capital, the business' lifespan and potential future sale, and family inheritance.

The most common structures available in the UK are outlined below with their primary advantages and disadvantages. Other countries have similar business types.

Common business types in the UK

Business type	Advantages	Disadvantages
Sole trader	• Privacy • Easy to start • Simpler accounting and tax	• Personal insolvency risk • Inability to raise investment capital • Potentially higher taxation
Partnership	• Privacy • Easy to start • Simpler accounting and tax	• Personal insolvency risk • Inability to raise investment capital • Potentially higher taxation • Reliance on old legislation
Limited liability partnership	• Easy to start • Lower personal insolvency risk	• Difficult to raise investment capital • Potentially higher taxation • Potentially higher compliance costs • More complex compliance
Limited company	• Easy to start • Lower personal insolvency risk • Flexible investment options • Tax breaks for investors	• Potentially higher compliance costs • Public domain • More complex compliance

Sole trader

By default, if you do nothing else but trade with the intention of making a profit, you will be a sole trader.

Advantages: Privacy, easy to start, simpler accounting and tax.

As a sole trader, your business accounts are private. The only people who will know how well you're doing (besides you) are the tax authorities and your accountant.

This kind of business is simple to start and operate – sometimes too simple. It's so simple that you can all too easily mix your business transactions with your personal transactions in the same bank account.

You should always create a separate business bank account in your name. And if your turnover exceeds the value-added tax (VAT) threshold (£85,000 in 2018), register for VAT. If your sales are largely to VAT-registered businesses and you have significant capital assets to acquire, it may be beneficial to register for VAT even when you're below the VAT threshold.

Another advantage of operating as a sole trader is that if you have initial tax losses, you can set them against other income from previous years, perhaps a former spell of employment, to potentially obtain tax refunds.

As a sole trader, you generally only need to create a profit-and-loss account for the tax authorities, and you're taxed on the total profits at your personal income tax rate. The accounting is therefore fairly straightforward.

Disadvantages: Personal insolvency risk, inability to raise investment capital, potentially higher taxation.

If you operate as a sole trader, you as an individual are at risk should the business go wrong. Say you operate in the construction industry and follow an architect's plans but the work proves to be badly designed. You could be personally liable for the rework, which could lead to insolvency. You might have insurance, but not all business risks are insured.

As a sole trader, you are a 100% owner of the business. There's no way to split you up and sell shares in the business to potential investors. It's therefore impossible to raise investment capital.

The tax you pay is calculated on your total profits, irrespective of how much you've reinvested in the business, so in general, for growing businesses that reinvest their profits, the overall tax on the business will be higher.

STRUCTURE YOUR BUSINESS APPROPRIATELY

A former director of an agricare multinational public limited company left his well-paid employment post to become an entrepreneur. His business would import a specialist chemical from the United States to transform cattle farming in the UK. He predicted the business would see a slow start with initial losses before becoming significantly profitable.

He started up as a sole trader, as most of the early phase involved building his profile. He was able to obtain tax refunds by setting his early-stage losses against his higher-rate employment earnings prior to starting his new business venture.

Unfortunately, the business never actually made it, but he did mitigate his investment with tax refunds.

STRUCTURE YOUR BUSINESS CORRECTLY

Many authors are specialists in a particular field and write in addition to their main job. Often, these authors write books using their name and have royalties paid to them personally.

But this leads to tax being charged at a higher rate. It also restricts opportunities for collaboration with potential partners. We encourage these kinds of clients to ensure the contracts with the publishing companies are in the name of a limited company, owned by them.

Depending on the circumstances, this can lead to a build-up of cash in the limited company, which is taxed at the lower corporate tax rate rather than higher income tax rates. By setting up the ownership this way at the start, you can also involve business partners by using the appropriate share structure.

Partnership

Advantages: Privacy, easy to start, simpler accounting and tax.

Why would you create a partnership? Mostly because it's simple to start and you can focus on business rather than legal issues at the beginning.

A partnership is similar to a sole trader except that you trade in conjunction with a business partner. Although it's a partnership, having a formal agreement is highly recommended, though there is no legal requirement to have one, and many partnerships exist without written legal agreements.

Historically, professional practices had no option but to create partnerships, and largely because of that many partnerships still exist today.

Partnership tax is similar to the tax for sole traders, all the business profits are calculated and then allocated to each partner based on their profit share. Each partner will be given a tax form that represents their share of the profits. That is then submitted to the tax authorities to calculate their personal tax.

Disadvantages: Personal insolvency risk, inability to raise investment capital, potentially higher taxation, reliance on old legislation.

On the risk side, you are jointly and severally liable for the business debts with your partner, with no limit. That means should there be an error in judgement or an uninsured claim, the partner with the most assets could suffer the most if the other partner's assets are used up in settling the claim.

For example, if solicitor partners J and S, with personal assets of £100,000 and £1,000,000 respectively, suffer an uninsured claim of £1,000,000 against their partnership, then J would pay £100,000 and S £900,000 to settle the claim. J still owes S £400,000 but doesn't have any assets to pay S – so the partner with the most assets loses the most.

Raising capital in a partnership is easier because you can sell a portion of the business. However, the nature of a partnership usually means that the management of the business cannot be split from the ownership, so investment-only capital from 'sleeping partners' is not attractive to investment partners.

In the same way as a sole trader's, *all* of a partnership's profits are subject to taxation, so partnerships intending to reinvest and grow will generally pay more tax than a limited company that reinvests. The reinvested element of profits would only suffer tax at the lower corporate tax rate rather than the potentially much higher personal income tax rate.

If no formal partnership agreement exists then the law governing the business is the Partnership Act of 1890.

My advice is to always have a written signed partnership agreement. The consequences of not having one are as follows:

- **Profit split** – In the absence of an agreement, profits are divided equally between the partners, which could lead to problems if one partner has contributed more than the other.

- **End of the partnership** – Any partner can at any time dissolve the partnership with immediate effect by giving notice to the other partners. In this case, all assets must be sold and all debts must be paid.

- **Death** – If a partner dies, the effects are the same as above. The entire business has to be sold and its debts paid.

- **Expulsion** – Without a partnership agreement, it's not possible to expel an individual partner. The only solution is to end the partnership, selling assets and settling debts immediately. If the other partners wanted to continue it would cause severe disruption; at worst, all the trade and business value could be lost.

WHEN A PARTNERSHIP CAN BE USEFUL

I dealt with a professional partnership of two equal partners. On a number of occasions, we considered incorporating the business. But every time we reviewed the situation, the partnership remained.

The circumstances were that trade was highly volatile and often the partners withdrew more money than the profits of the business. Because of the accounting rules for goodwill, they appeared insolvent.

Partnerships allow privacy, which in this case helped the continued trade. Their bankers still had full information and charges over personal assets. The tax authorities also had access to their business accounts, but crucially they were not in the public domain. Had they incorporated, they would have had restrictions on dividends and paid higher tax rates. Unusual, but it shows there are no hard and fast rules.

Limited liability partnership (LLP)

Advantages: Easy to start, lower personal insolvency risk.

This is a relatively recent corporate structure. It's an extension of the partnership concept and offers limited liability. It is taxed in the same way as a partnership but restricts the liability of the partners to balances on the capital and current accounts of the business. The trade-off is that the accounts must be filed on the public record at Companies House. For smaller businesses, the level of detail on the public record can be minimal and exclude much of the performance information. As businesses grow, more information, including turnover and profits, has to be made public.

The underlying principal of limited liability is that in exchange for limited liability you have to disclose your financial information to third parties.

Disadvantages: Difficult to raise investment capital, potentially higher taxation, potentially higher compliance costs, more complex compliance.

LLPs and partnerships raise capital in similar ways, so an investor becomes a partner in an LLP. Although there is no limit to the number of partners an LLP can have, in practice, there are usually no more than 1,000 members. All members are usually involved in the management of the business. If you plan to raise funds from the public or investors that don't want to be directly involved, an LLP is not an appropriate structure.

Similar to sole traders and partnerships, in an LLP, all profits are subject to taxation. LLPs intending to reinvest and grow will generally pay more tax than a limited company that reinvests.

LLPs have to follow the Companies Act whereas partnerships have much simpler accounting rules. This will invariably lead to higher professional fees as a result of the increased disclosure of the business' financial results.

LLP red tape is also increased, more accounting rules, extra forms for changes in partners/members, a requirement to file on public record an annual confirmation statement.

Limited company

Advantages: Easy to start, lower personal insolvency risk, flexible investment options, tax breaks for investors.

A limited company is easy to set up; it can be done online very quickly. A human being takes nine months to develop in the womb, but you can probably create a company in ninety minutes at a push. It will have many of the legal rights that a human has as soon as it's formed.

A limited company is a separate legal entity and has its own separate identity. It consists of managers (directors) and owners (shareholders). The word 'limited' refers to the liability of the shareholders, which is restricted to the amount of capital in the company. This enables investors to have certainty about the amount that they're investing in the business. They know exactly how much they could lose.

Because the management is separate from the shareholders, the business can raise capital through investors who have no interest in the day-to-day running of the business.

In its most basic form, a limited company will have at least one director and one shareholder, which could be the same person. The amount of capital can be as low as £1 and has no theoretical limit. One of the largest limited companies in the UK is household name John Lewis plc, which in 2018 had total capital in excess of £2.3 billion.[2]

Almost all limited companies are limited by shares. Each company has capital split into a number of shares, each of which represents a percentage of ownership. The exception to this is charitable organisations, which are usually limited by guarantee, meaning that they are usually set up as a legal entity to hold assets and have members who agree to pay a nominal sum toward any shortfall if they are wound up.

There are various types of shares. The common ones are ordinary voting, ordinary non-voting and preference shares. It's possible to create complex investment structures to fulfil the needs of most types of investor. Investors are paid dividends as a return on their investment.

---

2   Financial report 2018 at: www.johnlewispartnership.co.uk/content/dam/cws/pdfs/financials/our-year-1718/jlp-annual-report-and-accounts-2018-finance-report.pdf

A complex structure combines different share types. All companies will start with ordinary shares, which will have voting rights. However, when they want to raise further capital, they may issue a new group of shares with rights different to those of original ordinary shares. They could, for example, be entitled to the first tranche of profits. Another example might entail shares having income rights, but no voting rights. By mixing and matching various rights a company can create a complex structure tailored to their needs. But the more complex the structure becomes, the harder it could be to raise further capital, so you should always seek professional advice.

In the UK, the government often gives tax breaks through the Enterprise Investment Scheme (EIS) or the Seed Enterprise Investment Scheme (SEIS) (for smaller entities). Tax breaks encourage investment in entrepreneurial business and incentivise the UK economy. A higher-rate tax payer can invest £1,000 in an appropriate limited company at a cost of only £700. (There is more information on this in the 'Financing your idea' section in Chapter 3.)

Disadvantages: Potentially higher compliance costs, public domain, more complex compliance.

With all the flexibility and choice comes a degree of complexity and increased red tape. Limited companies must follow a prescribed legal format for their financial statements and deliver them to the public record within certain time limits (normally nine months after the period end). Limited companies have their own tax regime for corporate tax returns along with their own time limits. Once limited companies grow beyond prescribed size limits, they become subject to statutory audit and increased disclosure in the public domain.

A small company (less than £10.2m) need only disclose the bare minimum about their performance; once a company becomes medium sized, it needs to place significantly more information about its annual performance in the public domain.

The rules governing the running of the company are known as the articles of association and are agreed by shareholders, directors and the company secretary. A newly formed company will usually adopt default articles. Although default articles are useful, they do not cover many situations that are likely to arise during the life of the business. Shareholders do fall out, and it would be wise to have a shareholder agreement, which is not a default option, alongside the articles, to govern how disputes would be handled.

The most common scenario I encounter is in small to medium-sized enterprises (SMEs), where the directors and shareholders are the same. If one director falls out with the other(s) and they decide to split, there is no mechanism for the leaving director to be forced to sell their shares.

A shareholder agreement allows this mechanism to be agreed while everyone is on good terms, with a valuation method which is fair to all, rather than having a lengthy (and costly) legal dispute after the event.

Groups

When companies grow and diversify, it's common for groups to be created. Groups allow you to spread and ring-fence business risk across several companies, commonly known as subsidiaries. The main company, generally known as a holding company, owns more than 50% of the voting rights in each subsidiary.

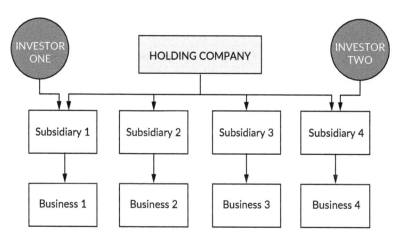

In the simple holding company structure shown above, each subsidiary could constitute a separate business unit. Perhaps Subsidiary 1 could be an airline business, Subsidiary 2 could be a music business, and Subsidiary 3 could be a media business. Each one could have a separate management team of directors, and indeed could have a proportion of different investors. If trading proves difficult in one subsidiary, it can be ring-fenced from the others. All profits can be passed up to the holding company in proportion to the shares it owns. This will incur extra costs, but it will help control risk, and allow diversification.

For example, Virgin Group has an overall holding company which invests as a shareholder in other Virgin companies. If, as an investor, you're interested in aviation or travel, you may want to invest in Virgin Atlantic but not Virgin Media. If one of the trading companies suffers problems, the others won't necessarily be affected.

Early on, consider how your business is likely to develop and clarify its potential needs to determine the most appropriate structure, which will govern how the business is taxed. Often an existing arrangement could be changed to commercially improve the business.

STRUCTURE YOUR BUSINESS CORRECTLY TO RAISE FUNDS

An ambitious entrepreneur came to me several years ago with an idea to import specialist drinks from around the world and sell them wholesale in the UK and Europe. Initially the entrepreneur had little of his own capital, but he did have the drive and vision to implement his ideas.

An initial investor offered some seed capital. By forming a limited company, the entrepreneur could give his investor a share in his business: £50,000 for 10% of the business. The entrepreneur retained 90% control. As the business grew, there was a need to obtain further funds, and the entrepreneur was able to sell more shares in return for further investment. This time, the price per share was higher. Further growth meant further funding, and recently the company raised further capital through selling shares on Crowdcube (a crowdfunding platform) at an even higher valuation. The price per share for the last raise valued the total company at £3 million, although it had only started five years previously.

The investors were also able to obtain significant tax benefits. Their cost of investment was reduced through SEED EIS and EIS.

The business structure you choose can enhance or hinder your future growth. You should consult a qualified chartered accountant before finalising any decision on the legal structure of your business.

Take it seriously

An adviser is critical

Research shows that businesses that have strong relationships with qualified professional advisers are much more likely to succeed.

In a recent study by Xero, a cloud accounting software provider, 2,000 current and former owners of businesses with twenty or fewer employees in the US and the UK were questioned. The Xero *Make or Break* report examined the differing experiences and attitudes of those whose companies had remained solvent and those who had had to shut their doors.[3] The report revealed that for those owners who collaborate with an adviser, 42% of survivors describe their relationship as excellent, compared to 27% of those whose company failed.

Any survivor knows that finding a great adviser isn't easy (you need to trust the adviser, and the adviser needs to care about your business), but once you find one, business becomes more rewarding – a problem shared is a problem halved!

Why is working with an adviser so important? By outlining your vision and goals to a third party, you become accountable, and will therefore strive to achieve the targets that you've set. If you have an adviser, you will also benefit from a third-party viewpoint.

A different viewpoint

It's easy to become so heavily involved in the day-to-day workings of your business that you get sucked

---

3   www.xero.com/content/dam/xero/pdf/Xero-Make-or-break-report.pdf

into doing the wrong things rather than keeping on track with your ultimate goals. For example, it's all too easy to be busy doing non-strategic technical tasks and wasting valuable time that could be spent on strategic tasks. At the beginning of the relationship with your adviser, you should meet regularly and have an agenda to ensure you create and stick to an appropriate plan for your success.

In 99% of businesses this isn't done, usually because it's perceived as a luxury or too expensive. But consider the following quote from Red Adair (an oil well firefighter who was a great innovator in his field): 'If you think it's expensive to hire a professional to do the job, wait until you hire an amateur.' Build in time with an adviser as a key part of your business plan, and develop your sales pricing to include this (instead of seeing it as an extra cost).

Clients I work with on an active basis always do better, and often smash their goals. One manufacturing client based in South East England went from a ten-year history of averaging £30,000 net profit to just under £1 million net profit over three years, by focusing on their goals and taking action to improve small things. Specifically, they focused on delivery performance and rejections. In doing so, customer experience, revisions to work, quality control and referrals were all improved.

The consequences of this improvement were life changing for so many people. The employees had job security and pride in their work, and the owners were in a position to pass on the business to the next generation and enjoy retirement.

I've been in the entrepreneurial world for over twenty-five years. I don't profess to know everything, but there aren't many common problems I haven't seen. You need someone with similar experience on your team, either as a full-time resource or as a part-time resource that you can call on as required. While it will cost money, think of it as an investment that will provide a great return.

THREE

Consider Cash Flow

Financing your idea

Before embarking on this step, it's important to do an initial assessment to determine whether the business is, theoretically, going to create financial profits for you and value for your customers. Knowing your basic funding requirements, you can then consider sources.

The first question is this: does your idea need capital funding or working capital funding? Or both? Capital funding is longer term and used to finance assets. Working capital funding supports your day-to-day operations.

Service-based businesses often require little capital funding, whereas manufacturing businesses often require significant funding for capital equipment at the outset *and* working capital to fund component purchases, stocks, customer debts, etc. The general rule of thumb is to match the length of funding to the nature of the asset being purchased. For example, a piece of plant equipment with a useful life of five years could be financed by debt with a term of five years. This is an example of capital funding.

Funding is either internal or external. There are hybrid versions of these two types, but most funding falls into these broad categories (see the 'Sources of finance' table on p52).

Outlined below are the main options available to entrepreneurs in the SME sector, roughly in order of common usage now, though the advancement of technology is likely to change this. Banks need to react much more quickly to the changing needs of the business community.

Internal funding

Personal wealth (debt or equity)

If you intend to use your own funds, you can introduce them either as debt or equity. If the business plan shows early-year losses, it could be tax efficient to start as a sole trader (make the losses) and obtain a tax repayment. When you start to become profitable, incorporate the business and reinvest future profits at a lower corporate tax rate. Each case needs to be considered on its own merits.

Family/friends (debt or equity)

These are usually 'softer' loans, by which we mean that the terms and conditions are usually less stringent than with other types of loan, but recipients of this kind of funding are often more diligent about repayment, as they are likely to be under an emotional obligation to ensure repayment. Unless the lender is in for the life of the business, the money should be introduced as a loan, with the terms and interest charges specified in a written loan agreement.

With all loans there will be a risk that the business may fail. To reduce the risk, the lender could also be given a legal charge over assets of the business, so that if the business does not succeed, the lender can at least take possession of these assets.

If the lender is in for the long term, and would like to see a profit when the business is sold, share capital might be more appropriate. If the company is profitable enough, the lender could then earn ongoing income from dividends.

Sources of finance

Debt	Equity
Personal wealth	Personal wealth
Family/friends	Family/friends
Credit cards	Retained profits
Bank overdraft	Active investment partner
Bank loans	Angel investment
Supplier credit	Crowdfunding
Asset funding	Mezzanine
Factoring	
Crowd-funded loans	
Customer advances	
Cloud-based direct ledger	
Specialist lending	

If you don't have access to internal sources of funding, you can look to external funding.

External funding

Equity vs debt financing

Difference	Equity	Debt
Ownership	Part of the business is sold	No change in business ownership
Exit	Investor sells shares at market price to recoup investment and return – no repayment by the business required	Loan must be repaid by the business at some point

(Continued)

Difference	Equity	Debt
Cost	A percentage of the total equity	An interest charge
Process	Create an investor pack with business plan, market analysis, cash flow forecasts	Complete a loan application
Personal guarantees	Not required	Usually required by lenders
Credit score	May be required	Will be used to set the level of interest – the lower the credit score, the higher the interest rate

Equity

Equity involves selling a part of the business and potentially reducing your control. This type of funding is long term in nature and is generally realised by the sale of part or all of the business in the future for a profit. Depending on the structure of the business, the equity holder often has voting rights regarding certain decisions and will own a percentage of the business. Equity holders may obtain a return on their capital from dividends taken from the profits that the business has made. The higher the profits, the higher the dividend can be. If there are no reserves, then there is nothing to distribute, and there won't be any dividends.

Tax incentives for investors

In many countries, governments offer tax incentives to encourage investment in business, which helps to promote national economic growth. The UK has several tax incentives, but the most common for SME entrepreneurs is the EIS; it allows investors to gain tax relief when they make the investment (UK 2017/18: 30%). There are a number of conditions regarding the use of EIS for business, largely in place to ensure the investment is genuine rather than some form of tax avoidance. Effectively, the investor pays seventy pence in the pound and the government pays the thirty pence balance, through the tax system.

In the UK, most trades will qualify. However, the following are specifically excluded:

- Coal or steel production
- Farming or market gardening
- Leasing activities
- Legal or financial services
- Property development
- Running a hotel
- Running a nursing home
- Power generation

There are also limits as to how much can be raised. Currently, the maximum is £5 million in any twelve months and £12 million during the lifetime of your company.

SEIS is the junior version of EIS. The government will pay 50% of your investment. The limit on investment is £150,000 and your company must be less than two years old. The trade exclusions are similar to those set out by the EIS.

For the social enterprise there is another variant, known as Social Investment Tax Relief (SITR). Your organisation must have a defined and regulated social purpose in order to benefit.

Tax relief is all very well, but how do you find the appropriate investors? The ability to find investors for any particular project, as you may expect, has changed dramatically over the last few years as a result of web-based technology, and it continues to develop. Today a number of crowdfunding platforms do the job of linking businesses to investors.

Equity crowdfunding

Businesses such as Crowdcube and Syndicate Room provide platforms to link your business to potential investors. In exchange for investment, you offer a percentage of the equity in the business.

As soon as you start raising equity funds, you need to consider your existing shareholders and their rights before executing your plan.

Always ensure you have the consent of the existing shareholders before pursuing this option. As with all equity investment, existing shareholders have pre-emption rights, which means they have the right to prevent their share of the business from being reduced by taking up their percentage of any new share offer.

A few years ago, I helped a business which had over-sold its initial investment proposition. The company had raised seed capital by agreeing to £40,000 for 10% of the company. The investor (Mr A) understood that he would always have 10%. When it came to a further round of funding, the company wanted to offer a further 20% of the company for £100,000 by increasing the number of shares on offer. However, that would dilute the shares of Mr A and go against the initial deal. To avoid any problems, the managing director bought out the original contract so that Mr A would have no special rights and the company was free to raise further funds. Subsequently, the company had a further funding round valuing the business at £3.5 million.

The following example highlights what should happen.

A company has 10,000 shares of £1 in issue split equally among four shareholders (£2,500 each). The shares were issued two years ago. The company has spotted an opportunity for growth that requires further investment in machinery. It wants to raise £150,000 and is willing to issue another 2,000 shares at £75 each to the new investors.

Two thousand shares is 16.67% (2,000/12,000) of the post-investment shares. Now, the entire business is valued at £900,000 (12,000 × £75). Any existing 25% shareholder must be offered the opportunity to purchase their existing percentage of the new issue at the offer price of £75 each, ie £37,500 (pre-emption). If they refuse and waive their rights, a third party may then purchase them.

After the capital has been raised, the initial investors who waived their rights to buy would each have 2,500 shares of 12,000 (20.833%), compared to their original 25% of the company before the investment round. The overall value of the initial investors' share has not changed, it's just that they now own a smaller percentage of a company that is more valuable overall.

Overlooking the pre-emption offer is a breach of company law. In the example above, the value of the shares has gone up dramatically and the existing shareholders may well be satisfied with that growth, but they must always be offered the chance to retain their existing percentage. It is possible to change the individual company rules (articles of association) to simplify this, but that should only be done following specific legal advice.

MAKING CROWDFUNDING WORK FOR YOU

Earlier, we looked at a client in the drinks industry who founded his company in 2010. He started on his own in the corner of the local station farmers' market, with two shelves of retail space. He now has bars in London, Canterbury and Margate, and a wholesale import operation dealing with over 800 customers across the UK.

To grow as quickly as it has, the company used crowdfunding via Crowdcube and the government's enterprise incentive scheme to make investing in its business more attractive. At each round of EIS, it needed clearance from HMRC to ensure investors would get tax relief for their investments.[4]

There are a few prerequisites for equity crowdfunding using UK platforms.

- The business must be a UK or Irish limited company (not an LLP or sole trader)

- The business can't be involved in anything of a sexual nature, property development, or filmmaking/theatrical productions

- The business must have a valid, active Companies House number

---

4   www.bottle.shop/pages/about

You will also need to produce the following:

- The structure of the company (if the business consists of a group structure, the funds must be raised for the top company – ensure the company number for the top company is provided)

- Existing shareholders, and if there are any majority institutional shareholders, the terms of their investments (this will cover pre-emption rights, as explained above)

- The director's corporate and financial CV

With equity crowdfunding, you will be accountable to third-party shareholders. You will need to provide commentary to those shareholders on the trading of the business after the new investment.

To successfully raise finances, you must hone your pitch to perfection, whether you present it face to face, through a written document or via an online video. Given the ease with which video can be created and distributed today, this is rapidly becoming the most common medium.

Debt

Debt is funding that must be repaid, and it can place a significant burden on the business. It can vary from short-term overdrafts to long-term mortgages or debentures. Generally, a business needs to repay debt over a term and will pay interest for the benefit of using the funds. Interest payments are not usually dependent upon the business making a profit. Interest is usually tax deductible. The 'Sources of equity' table shows common forms of debt.

In my experience, businesses often don't understand the ramifications of bad planning when it comes to deciding on funding. It is common for entrepreneurs to chase capital funding at any cost and pay dearly later. This is another area where external advice can help change the business fundamentally.

I have recently had to help two different businesses extricate themselves from expensive funding. One was being charged an annual interest rate of 98% for his loan. The other was being charged interest on debt he hadn't actually used because of a minimum-usage charge in his funding arrangement.

Cutting corners with business practices can significantly affect cash flow and, consequently, the funding requirement – for example, not having a system for chasing outstanding invoices. This was the case for one of our clients when we started working with them. They were regularly hitting their overdraft limit and had to spend time trying to obtain extended payment terms from their suppliers. This meant they wasted lots of time on totally unnecessary administration and were suffering unnecessary bank charges and bank interest. We helped them understand the consequences of this practice, and then helped them implement a debt-chasing system which was both automated and customised. This had the result of turning an overdraft into a consistent £50,000 positive balance in the bank. The director then had less stress and more time to think about strategic planning and running the business. No external working capital funding was required. All they needed to do was retrain their customers to pay on time.

In the modern era of cloud computing, all businesses should be taking advantage of the tools and techniques available to help them grow.

When it comes to raising debt finance, the most common forms are outlined below, alongside some more innovative ideas.

Credit cards

These should be used only for short-term needs. And when it comes to funding your business, use a business credit card rather than a personal one. I've seen so many instances where businesses cannot obtain the appropriate tax relief because of inadequate recordkeeping with a personal credit card. The balance should be paid off in full monthly. There are often fringe benefits to using business credit cards, especially if you pay them off in full every month. For example, some banks give air miles based on spend. Even if all you are doing is a normal monthly spend, you could pick up some personal tax-free air miles.

Bank overdraft

Almost all entrepreneurs have a bank overdraft, and as long as it's used correctly, it's a reasonably cheap and flexible form of funding. There are some key points to note, though. It's almost always repayable on demand, though in practice this happens rarely. An overdraft usually requires a personal guarantee from the directors, which means the bank can obtain any shortfall of funds from the directors should the business fail, even if it's a limited company.

A bank overdraft should be used only for monthly/quarterly cycles of cash flow. That means you should be returning to a positive balance every business cycle. (The business cycle is governed by a combination of your terms and conditions with customers, suppliers and employees.) If that isn't happening, it's an indicator that you aren't profitable enough. If you have a permanent overdraft, you need to consider alternative funding.

Bank loans

Bank loans are commonly used to fund capital purchases and should match the life of the asset being purchased. This way, when it's time to replace the asset, you're able to take out a new loan. Bank loans typically come with an arrangement fee and a variable interest rate (generally a number of percentage points above the base rate) and are often, but not always, secured on a specific asset. In general, the more security the bank has, the cheaper the interest rate. When obtaining a bank loan, ensure that the asset you're buying will produce enough return to repay the loan, the interest and the costs of using the asset and still give you a profit.

Supplier credit

Supplier credit involves negotiating appropriate credit terms with your suppliers before dealing with them and then sticking to those terms. Delaying payment to a supplier after you've received the service without credit terms in place isn't conducive to a good future business relationship.

At the beginning of a supplier relationship, the salesperson you're negotiating with will likely be keen to make the sale, so at this point you can ask for, and in many cases receive, favourable payment terms. In my experience, almost all suppliers will offer better-than-standard payment terms if the question is asked. I've seen it work for all the main business suppliers, for example, stock suppliers, stationery suppliers and furniture and plant suppliers – the main exception is utilities. Negotiating credit terms fairly at the start of a relationship with a supplier can significantly reduce the amount of other funding required.

Asset funding

This type of funding is similar to a bank loan but is secured to the asset (commonly vehicles or large items such as plant and machinery) the lender is funding. If repayments are missed, the lender usually takes title of the asset. As with bank funding, you need to consider the whole deal before going ahead. Will the asset produce enough income to warrant the repayments and interest charges? Because the lender has security over an asset, it's much less likely that they will ask for a personal guarantee, and you should refuse signing one at the outset if possible. The lending is usually done by a salesperson who will go all out to get the deal signed, including waiving the need for a personal guarantee.

Factoring/invoice discounting

Factoring or invoice discounting both involve raising finance based on the value of your customer invoices; you receive payment as soon as the invoice is raised rather than when the customer pays.

The difference between factoring and invoice discounting comes down to the degree to which your customer is aware of the form of finance.

In general terms, a funder will provide a factoring facility, which is a percentage of the amount of customer debt owed to the business. If you have total customer debts of £1 million, inclusive of VAT, a factoring funder will typically offer you between 60% and 80% of the amount due, ie between £600,000 and £800,000, in cash, which you can use as working capital for your business.

For factoring, your customer will usually know that you have factored the debt and will pay the factor directly. At that point, the factor will then pay you the remaining percentage.

With invoice discounting, the cash flow benefits are similar, in that the invoice discounting provider pays you as soon as the invoice is raised, and your customer will pay your business under their normal terms (eg, 30 days). You then effectively repay the funder. In practice you then update your customer ledgers and the funder will adjust the funding facility to reflect the current available funding across all of your customers. At any given time they will give you the agreed percentage of the balance outstanding from your customers.

Over the years I've encountered variations on the above, but the principles are the same. Finance charges are usually charged in several parts, built up as follows:

- A charge for the facility (say 0.5%) even if not used

- A charge for drawing down the available funds (typically 0.75% to 1.0%)

- Bank transfer fees (higher for same day, lower for three days)

The overall costs of this type of funding can become quite significant. You must also normally commit to a minimum contract period (usually twelve months).

Normally, you're given a maximum amount that you can finance with each customer (credit limit). If your customers are private individuals, they are unlikely to be given credit limits. If you deal largely with large business customers with strong credit ratings and intend to grow quickly with strong margins, then this could well be the most appropriate method for you.

A word of warning, though!

If your large business customers' credit ratings suddenly fall or your sales drop, your funding will drop too. And this could be when you need the funding most. The funders can also turn off funding for specific customers at their discretion. Both of these things have led to the sudden collapse of business. The funders will recover customer advances that subsequently become bad debts

Factoring/invoice discounting is best avoided unless your client base is strong, stable and spread across many customers.

Crowdfunding

Crowdfunding involves obtaining funding from many (a crowd) and repaying the funders with interest. It's also commonly referred to as peer-to-peer lending. The source of the loan is usually an internet platform which connects businesses with potential lenders and cuts out the traditional large-bank middleman.

The basic requirement is usually two to three years of trading history, so it's not generally appropriate for a start-up. But for a business that has been running profitably for a few years, crowdfunding can be a great way to raise funds for further growth, usually offering relatively quick decisions on the amounts to be loaned by lenders and keen interest rates compared to those of the high street banks (though high street banks are improving all the time).

Customer advances

Another source of capital is customers! Depending on your product or service, you may be able to set terms that remove the working capital headaches. If you import goods, for instance, why not ask a customer for a deposit, which could finance your deposit to your supplier?

If you provide an annual service, perhaps ask your customer to pay throughout the year, rather than once at the end of the year. It might sound trivial, but the difference to your cash flow could be radical.

The most important thing in this case is to establish your terms at the beginning of your relationship with your customer and ensure the customer is in agreement. I have transformed my business by breaking away from industry norms and making processes much easier and more transparent for customers.

We don't charge by the hour – we price all work up front and our customers pay smaller monthly amounts rather than a large, unknown time-based bill delivered long after the work has been done. We also don't charge extra charges for telephone calls; we encourage clients to bring us their problems so we can help them more!

It's hard to believe how many legal and finance professionals still surprise their customers with terrifyingly large bills based on how long it took them to do something. The slower they are, the higher the fee. Only snails would vote for that.

Cloud-based direct ledger

A relatively new concept, this is a variant of factoring, with many of the advantages and few of the drawbacks. Cloud-based direct ledger financing involves selling invoices to a market on an *individual* basis for a discount rate.

For example, let's say you have an invoice of £100,000 for work done for a creditworthy customer. You could auction this invoice on a peer-to-peer market and gain instant financing on the invoice for up to 90% (£90,000) within twenty-four hours; you'll receive the remainder less the fees when your customer pays. The fee depends on the auction and customer's credit rating, but could be around 5%. This might sound expensive, but if built into your pricing and used sparingly, it could be an effective way to obtain working capital. Most of these providers expect a direct feed into your online accounts system so that they can monitor your financial health in real time.

Specialist lending

Many industries have specialist lenders, and depending on your industry, they may be the best source of funding for you. These lenders understand your industry, which is a benefit, but they often charge a premium for the value of their understanding.

Ultimately, all of these lenders want to lend your business money for a return on theirs.

Day-to-day cash flow control

Once you've raised your capital, the next step is to manage your day-to-day cash flow. You've probably heard the phrase 'cash is king'. There is some truth in that statement, but I prefer the analogy that cash is the lifeblood of all business. If a human runs out of blood, all their organs cease to function.

If a business runs out of cash, the business will cease to function.

The cash flow cycle

The diagram below shows an overview of the cash flow cycle. As a general rule, the faster the cycle, the less cash is required. If the cycle is slow, more cash will be required.

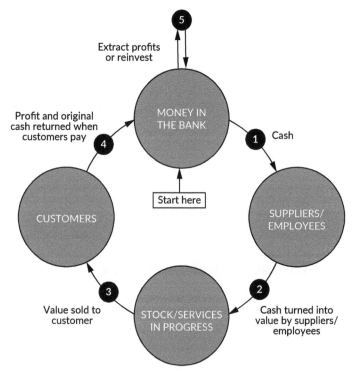

It's important to be able to visualise the cycle and understand the time involved in each step.

It all starts with value creation.

Step one

You commit to paying for production and labour. Payment can be made in advance or in arrears. Many employees and subcontractors can be paid monthly in arrears. Suppliers often give credit, though this is dependent on credit history and credit checks.

Step two

Your suppliers and employees create the value (either a service or a product). This could take a significant time (building a house) or be instantaneous (a download in the app store).

Step three

The customer decides to buy the service / product. The time involved here could be significant (eg, furniture, holidays, cars).

Step four

The customer pays.

The steps, along with how they add up to create your cash flow cycle, are outlined in the table below.

Cash flow cycle, day totals

Average number of days it takes customers to pay	X
Average number of days it takes before customers buy your stock/service (how long it's on the shelf)	Y
Average number of days it takes to produce your stock/service	Z
Less: Number of days from delivery to pay suppliers/employees	B
Length of cash flow cycle	A=X+Y+Z-B

If we put some figures into the cash flow table, we can work out the cash requirement. For the purposes of this exercise, we'll assume there's no VAT or general sales tax. Let's say your business' annual turnover is £1 million and the same level of business is conducted every day. It's an artificial example but will help explain the point.

You daily average will be £2,740 per day (£1 million/365 days). Assuming a 30% gross margin and an annual profit of £100,000, the daily cost of running the business, including salaries, would be (£900,000/365 days) £2,466.

Using typical UK business norms, the total cash flow cycle (A) can quite easily add up to ninety days. This would mean the business above would need £296,000 of working capital funding (see the cash flow predictor diagram opposite).

Annual turnover	£	1,000,000
Gross margin		30%
Annual cost of production/sales	£	769,231
Annual cost of overheads	£	130,769
Anticipated annual profit	£	100,000

Daily turnover	£	2,740

Daily cost of production/ sales including overheads	£	2,466

		Days		Cash
Average days it takes customers to pay	X	60	£	164,384
Average days it takes before customers buy your stock/ service once complete	Y	30	£	73,973
Average days it takes to produce your stock/service	Z	30	£	73,973
Less				
Number of days from delivery to pay suppliers/employees	B	120	£	295,890

		Days		Cash	
Length of cash/value cycle	X+Y+Z-B	0	£	16,438	Average cash finance required
Maximum cash required	(X+Y+Z)/B		£	295,890	Total cash funding requirement

Days of profit to fund business	1080.00

The cash flow predictor diagram above shows that it will take 1,080 days of retaining profits (excluding business taxes) to build enough cash reserves to run the business within these parameters. With this in mind, you can understand why managing X, Y and Z, and B is worth some effort.

So what can be done to manage the cash flow cycle? First, get rid of any preconceptions of what is and isn't possible.

Let's start with the customer payment days (X). In the UK, many businesses are accustomed to a cash flow cycle of sixty days. I have visited many businesses where they discuss customer payment days (X) being reduced from eighty days down to seventy days. While a reduction from eighty to seventy customer payment days certainly is an improvement, seventy days still creates massive headaches for whoever is managing the cash flow.

Strategies to reduce customer payment days (X)

Customer payment days is also commonly known as debtor days. It is often the longest part of a cash flow cycle. Below are several strategies to help reduce customer payment days.

- Establish your terms *at the outset*
    - Explain that you pay your bills on time and you only work with similarly minded customers
    - If appropriate (for long projects), ask for a deposit (which de-risks the deal and ensures commitment)
    - Consider whether instalments could be appropriate
    - Add a breach of payment terms penalty (30% for anyone who cheats the system) and pass this money on to a charity (we support B1G1)

- Make it easy to collect your amounts due

  - Offer payment by direct debit. If you use a cloud accounting system, you can automate collection via direct debit on your agreed due date for little more than your current bank charges

  - Offer payment by credit card

  - Provide your bank details on every invoice/statement

- Use an automated chasing system

  - Ensure every invoice is chased, without fail. Several cloud systems can do this for you, including Satago and Chaser (which are both excellent)

- Reward businesses that pay within your terms

  - Perhaps offer a prize draw for customers that pay on time

- Consider prompt-payment discounts

  - Think about raising your prices and then discounting heavily for prompt payment (settlement discounts work best if they are massive)

If for some reason you can't obtain terms that work for you, which can often happen when doing business with public-sector customers, consider invoice discounting, but build in a price premium to cover the cost of the financing.

By building a system from the beginning that minimises payment delays and manages customer payments, it's possible to have negative debtor days (ie, customers paying in advance). The best firms, including my own, have negative debtor days.

Strategies to reduce the sales cycle (stock days)

Stock days (Y) is the value of goods/services that have been completed but not yet sold expressed in days. For example, if a business has a cost value of £100,000 of stock in the warehouse, and it has a daily spend of £2,000, it has 50 days of stock.

The time it takes customers to buy your product or service once it's made available is a key factor in cash flow. Let's use a shoe shop as an example. This type of business has a high stock level requirement. For each style of shoe, a multitude of sizes is required. If the shop has 100 styles, it immediately needs at least 700 pairs of shoes in stock; if it sold 7 pairs a day, it would have 100 days' worth.

Twenty years ago, stock management options were limited. Today, many options exist, all centred on just-in-time stock management and creating demand in advance of service/stock production. Online businesses can now pass orders directly to their suppliers and then manage customers' expectations (clarify expected delivery dates). For example, Nike now delivers custom trainers in a few weeks; the customer pays on order and is told when to expect delivery. Nike has no cash tied up in the deal.

Commerce is ultimately the point at which supply meets demand. It's no good creating supply if there's no demand, and it's equally pointless creating demand if you can't supply. The key is to manage the intersection of supply and demand; doing so drives price and sales.

- Generate demand before your service/product is ready. Use marketing strategies to pre-sell your value.

  - Create a launch programme

  - Offer limited-edition products (like Apple)

  - Operate a waiting list (like Michelin-starred restaurants)

  - Keep your customers/prospects up to date on your next value proposition

- Set up a marketing system to do this systematically for each iteration of your ideas. Consider focused niche marketing, for example, specialising in false eyelashes, with the power of the internet you can specialise in very niche markets but sell right across the world in your chosen niche.

- Use an automated marketing and sales tracking system that integrates points of contact, and builds and hones your prospects' demands; Amazon is very good at this, letting you know that customers like you who have bought whatever you have just bought also bought this item – simple but effective.

- Ensure your conversion system, from prospect to customer, is simple and customer transparent: Netflix uses a simple FAQ system that answers many questions and leads a prospect to becoming a customer through linking to a sign-up process.

- Use a pricing system that maximises your value to the customer and explains that value to your customer: find out as much as possible about your customers to ensure that you are selling at the correct price point for them (consider the old-fashioned example of the gentleman's outfitter that always starts with the most expensive item and works down until they hit the correct price for the individual customer).

- Make it easy for the customer actually to buy your product: after all the effort to make the sale, ensure you can accept the transaction in as many forms as are appropriate for your customer. For example, if you are selling to private individuals, ensure you can take card payments; if you are selling houses, you need to have a suitable bank transaction system.

Use technology as much as possible to create and manage the demand/sales system.

Strategies to reduce the production cycle (production days)

The most effective tool to minimise the production cycle (Z) is automation. Why?

- It reduces human error

- It allows products and services to be delivered consistently, which ultimately creates a more favourable impression on the customer

- It allows you to objectively plan the production process

You could improve your bank by £386,000

If all the above strategies were used, the transformation would be monumental; for example, if the debtor days were converted to −15 (ie, payment two weeks in advance), the stock days were reduced to seven (one week), and value creation took three days. Leaving our payment days at thirty, which would be normal for a salaried service business, we would transform the cash flow requirement to an overall average of −35 days, which leads to a healthy bank balance averaging £90K, compared to an overdraft requirement for the same business of £296K, a £386K swing. The bad-debt risk would also be significantly lowered. What could you achieve in your business?

FOUR

Making Cloud Accounting Work For You

The entrepreneurs of today are in such a fortunate position with respect to the resources available to them. The plethora of cloud software resources has made an expensive and complex task (managing your business) much more straightforward and much less costly.

The last ten years have seen a comprehensive advancement of financial tools, marketing tools, and the ability to reach customers anywhere in the world 24/7. This period has also seen remarkable change in the accessibility and productivity of accounting systems. The modern-day entrepreneur can now collaborate much more effectively with suppliers, customers, advisers and financiers than ever before.

Imagine a world where your bank is integrated with your accounts system, which is integrated with your payment processing system, which is integrated with your collections system, which is integrated with your cloud reporting system, which is integrated with a desktop / tablet control system – and all in real time. You no longer have to imagine. The technology is available now.

Where do you start?

The first task is to establish the core of your business: the accounting system.

In the UK, options include Xero, QuickBooks, FreeAgent and Sage. These are the main market leaders, but this list isn't exhaustive.

The beauty of all four of the above is that they allow real-time access to your information. With a true picture of your finances, you're able to make meaningful decisions.

Used incorrectly, or by the wrong hands, tools can cause more harm than good, so it's important to consult suitably trained operators. I'm quite sure that if you gave me a hammer, nails and a shelf, the shelf would fall down immediately. Although all of the above are relatively easy to use, they are also relatively easy to set up incorrectly. I always advise speaking to a qualified accountant who is well versed in the system you choose.

So, what do you need to think about when setting up your accounting system?

- What types of reports are you expecting to generate? This will drive the design of the accounting core structure.

- Have you set up the appropriate shortcuts to make input quick, easy and accurate?

- If you sell products, have you set them up in the system correctly so that you know how much stock you have on hand and have sold?

- Is your bank cloud friendly? Most are, but a few still don't integrate. You need to be able to connect to your bank.

- Can you connect to other forms of payment systems (eg, direct debit systems, debtor-chasing systems)?

After establishing your core accounting system, you need to consider the add-on tools in the cloud ecosystem that surrounds this core.

At the time of writing there are over 700 apps in the Xero app store. These apps cover inventory and stock, payments management, CRM, time tracking, invoicing and jobs, point of sale, payroll, e-commerce, reporting, bills and expenses, better project tracking, financial services – the list goes on.

Not all apps are the same quality, and it's certainly useful to speak to existing users before utilising any of them. Some, however, you shouldn't be without.

Must-have apps

An app for invoice processing

Manually entering invoices into an accounting system and then filing the source document piece of paper should be a thing of the past. Instead, you can either scan or take a photograph of the invoice and process it with an accounting app. The app uses optical character recognition to translate the invoice and enter the details into the accounting system for you. Then it attaches a copy of the invoice to the transaction and files it within the accounting system. You can then drill down from the figures in the accounts to the transactions and subsequently find a copy of the invoice.

This type of app will transform your recordkeeping and allow you to take another step closer to a paperless system. Having electronically filed records is especially useful if you have a visit from tax inspectors. In fact, at one visit that we attended with a client, the tax officer was so impressed by the ease with which invoices could be found, they asked for a business card.

An app or direct feed that connects you to your bank

Once you're properly tracking your invoices, the next step is to link your bank to your accounting system. As noted, most (but not all) major banks have a direct feed from their online banking systems into the main cloud accounting systems. This produces a number of advantages for entrepreneurs.

- **Time saving** – You don't have to spend time organising statements and entering the details into your accounting systems

- **Accuracy** – All transactions come into your accounting system directly from the bank; no input errors

- **Completeness** – When you do things manually, it's easy to miss something, which then leads to time wasted trying to spot the difference

- **Quality improvements** – Instead of spending hours putting the numbers in, you can spend time overviewing your position in real time and consulting with advisers in a meaningful way, which ultimately improves your ability to manage the business and make relevant decisions; you have key information at your fingertips

An app to automate credit control

Many businesses spend vast amounts of time and effort chasing payments from customers. As I stressed earlier in Chapter 3, a short invoice-to-payment period is essential to maintaining positive cash flow and reducing funding requirements.

Several applications can be utilised in conjunction with your cloud accounting program to enable the automated chasing of debt. I've discussed why you should avoid offering credit, but in some industries and with some customers, it's inevitable. This is especially the case when dealing with the public sector. In time this will change, but you need solutions that work now.

Apps such as Satago and Chaser allow you to create a series of reminder letters which can be automatically sent to customers at specified intervals.

Clients who use these kinds of apps often go from overdraft to cash in the bank in a short space of time. Initially some are put off by the thought of losing customers as a result of chasing amounts outstanding. The key is to chase professionally. You will not lose a good customer if you chase in a business-like way with appropriate language at the appropriate time. If a customer is only using a business because of its relaxed credit terms, then there's a problem with that business' value proposition. After all, you're only chasing amounts which are contractually due to you.

With the tools outlined above in place, you can deal confidently with your numbers and manage your taxes.

FIVE

Follow The Rules

The common opinion of the population is that the tax inspector is a person to be despised. In reality, the individuals who work for Her Majesty's Revenue and Customs are, on the whole, normal, decent people. As in all walks of life, there are the odd extremes. Some tax inspectors can come across as overly officious and power crazed. The art of dealing with them is to stick to the facts. Tax law was written so the government could finance public spending. Since the recession of 2008, the UK government and many others around the world have found their finances under pressure. As a result, the government has become much more demanding and looks to retain cash wherever possible. In my experience, tax repayments have been taking longer and longer and involve much more red tape than was the case before 2008. As much as possible, avoid the need to rely on repayments from HMRC.

The best way to manage your taxes and other compliance issues is to obtain qualified expert advice. Do it upfront – don't wait until you have a problem!

DANGERS OF UNQUALIFIED ADVICE

I have numerous horror stories about taxes, as many businesses have come to me for advice after having taken the cheap option: of consulting unqualified tax advisers. One was told they didn't need to complete a tax return as they hadn't been sent one! Another was in such a mess the tax inspector opened a huge personal enquiry that went back six years.

Types of taxes

Taxes fall into the following categories.

Business tax

Businesses are taxed on profits made during the period in which they operate – usually annually. A business could be charged income tax, partnership tax or corporation tax, depending on its structure, and the percentages can range from 19% to 45%. The government is discussing the possibility of reducing the headline corporation tax rate to a much smaller figure in the future. In general, the more profitable a company is, the more business tax it will incur.

Employment tax

The government also charges tax based on the wage roll of the business. Currently this is 13.8% of amounts paid to employees. The government uses the term 'employer's national insurance' rather than 'tax' in this case. In addition, there are further taxes on the employees themselves; in the UK this is known as pay as you earn (PAYE) tax. The business is used as an unpaid tax collector for the government. PAYE can be as high as 45%.

Consumption tax

In the UK, consumption tax is known as VAT. In other countries, it's commonly referred to as general sales tax (GST).

VAT is added to the initial sales value and charged to your customers. You are required to charge VAT if your turnover exceeds £85,000 (2018).

For example, if you sell a widget for £100, the business needs to add VAT (20%), which will create a total value on the sales invoice of £120 (ie, £100 for the business and £20 for the government). At the end of the VAT period (usually a quarter), the business must complete an online return summarising all income and VAT and send the VAT payment to the government. If in the quarter the business has purchased goods with VAT, it can generally deduct the VAT on its business expenditures and reduce the amount payable at the end of the quarter. Again, the business is used as an unpaid tax collector.

Capital tax

In the UK, this is known as capital gains tax, and it's a tax on the increasing value of the business or its assets, such as property or investments. Depending on the type of business, this tax can range from 10% to 28% in the UK.

Avoid the tax pitfalls

As your business grows, you'll pay more tax. For every pound you spend in a profitable business, assuming the business makes a profit of 20%, the total tax could be as high as seventy-five pence in the pound. The popular press will have you believe that businesses such as Amazon and Google don't pay tax. However, they're only avoiding the business tax element and still pay around seventy pence to the exchequer through consumption tax (VAT) and employment-related taxes (PAYE/National Insurance).

It's impossible to avoid paying tax to the government, but what you can do is manage your affairs so as to pay only the minimum amount of tax you're legally required to pay. How do you do that?

You need to seek out as much tax relief as possible. For example, almost every entrepreneur has a mobile phone, but how many are claiming tax relief on the phone, which is specifically exempted from employment tax? Or claiming part of their home expenses if they work from home? Or taking advantage of the trivial benefits exemption which allows you to pay staff up to £50 at a time with no PAYE consequences? (It can't be paid in cash, though!) More reasons for choosing the right qualified accountant.

As discussed, the government has introduced schemes such as the EIS, which provides tax relief to investors who invest in small businesses. (See the 'External funding' section.)

EIS

Many of our clients have raised funds using EIS funding, which allows businesses to raise equity at a cost of seventy pence in the pound for the investor (fifty pence in the pound for SEED EIS). So that it works for both the business and the investor, we ensure all the relevant compliance forms are completed before any transactions take place, to remove any uncertainty. We then obtain outline approval from HMRC before proceeding with the fundraising.

If you set up a business using the correct structure, you can ensure that you pay only 10% capital gains tax rather than 20% by fulfilling the requirements for entrepreneur's relief. As companies grow, they can slip back from 10% to 20% by failing to qualify for entrepreneur's relief. If the business is worth £5 million, for example, the extra tax would be £500,000. So, make sure you review your capital gains tax situation at least annually.

PROTECT FUTURE RELIEFS

An entrepreneur had built up significant reserves (almost £5 million) in his successful limited company. As he had a limited company, his financial information was was disclosed at Companies House online, in the public domain. He started to receive feedback; his customers said his prices were too high, and his suppliers thought he should pay them more.

Because of the way taxation reliefs work, this also meant that the company could be classified as an investment company rather than a trading company, leading to higher taxation. Generally, capital gains tax is higher for an investment company than for a trading company.

By restructuring the business and splitting the trade and investment assets into two separate businesses, we were able to save our client over £200,000 in capital gains tax. He moved his trading business to a completely different company with much lower reserves and the £5 million ended up in a separate investment company and was no longer in plain sight of his customers or suppliers. The overall result for the client was a lower tax rate and a better commercial negotiating position.

Tax enquiries

Because of the government's need for cash, it has developed a targeted tax-enquiry regime. It's fairly simple: before getting a refund, you're likely to receive a visit or an enquiry letter from a tax inspector. Often these visits result in a delay of repayment, but if the company is badly managed, they can lead to penalties and extra tax. In my experience, a business which keeps good records and has a thorough trail of transactions will have nothing to fear from a visit from the tax inspector.

Top reasons for being selected for an enquiry

1. You have asked for a tax repayment

2. There has been a significant change in your trading profile (eg, sales have halved or doubled) with no obvious explanation

3. Your trading performance is different from those of similar businesses in your industrial classification

4. You have had an enquiry before and the outcome was such that the tax authorities perceive there is a risk of tax not being fully disclosed or paid (a polite way of saying you're on the heavy scrutiny list)

5. You are subject to a random check

6. You are a 'high net worth' individual and invited to join HMRC's High Net Worth Unit

Over the years I've seen hundreds of enquiries, ranging from simple checks of the facts to in-depth enquiries involving COP9 rules (suspicion of serious tax fraud), where tax inspectors have visited individuals' homes and threatened criminal action.

In recent years, the government has used psychologists to draft letters and word them in such a way as to nudge you to pay (and ultimately increase the overall tax take). Again, you need a qualified tax adviser that you can call on if you're an entrepreneur in business.

Remember, the government is just like any other business – it needs cash, and its main source is the taxpayer.

What happens during a tax enquiry?

Generally, step one involves ascertaining the facts and what actually happened during any transaction. Next, the applicable tax law is applied to the transaction and the tax is calculated. At this point there could be an element of subjectivity; negotiation may be required.

Finally, the tax authorities will make a decision. It then becomes a matter of whether you acted reasonably and disclosed all the facts. HMRC will either issue a penalty or an interest charge or will simply agree with how you have followed the tax rules to assess your tax. You will have the option to appeal or negotiate time to pay.

In almost all cases, we've helped our clients end up with a better result than they would have had if they had dealt with the enquiry on their own.

Just last month, we received a written apology from HMRC regarding a matter that had gone on for over eighteen months. Often, we succeed in having penalties removed or suspended. In the worst-case scenario, we obtain manageable time to pay arrangements so that the business can continue to grow and help the economy.

The key is to prepare the information for the tax authorities correctly, using the applicable tax law and maximising existing reliefs and allowances.

I haven't yet met a client who wants to pay more tax than is legally required. I also have many clients who just want peace of mind – to know that if there is a problem, they have someone to take it on for them.

Staying ahead of the legislation

Once you reach the turnover threshold of £85,000 per annum, you must register for VAT. At this point, you will have to charge an extra 20% VAT on top of your sales price (there are certain exceptions for some businesses). You also benefit by being able to reclaim the VAT that is charged to you.

The best way to manage VAT is to use a cloud accounting system that can track it for you. I also recommend having an accountant on hand to check the software has been correctly configured to account for VAT. Most cloud systems will prepare the VAT return for you and allow you to submit it from the software. VAT returns are due annually, monthly, or, most commonly, quarterly. Automate as much of the transaction recording process as possible, and ensure you use the most applicable VAT schemes. From April 2019, businesses must have their accounting systems digitally linked to HMRC to account for VAT. This is part of the government's initiative to collect tax more efficiently (known as Making Tax Digital).

Once VAT is under control, if you employ people, you will need to set up and operate a PAYE account for salaries and wages on a monthly basis. Again, automation is key here, and strong PAYE software systems will keep the process smooth and simple. Alongside PAYE is auto enrolment, which is now an automatic right for employees in the UK (subject to certain thresholds). The government needs people to provide for their time in retirement, and the current solution is auto enrolment, managed by employers, whereby employees have a percentage of their salary deducted to be saved in their individual tax-free savings pots for later life.

Having paid your VAT and your staff (which includes you if you're a director) throughout the year, at the end of the year it's time to calculate the business profits and the resultant tax on those profits. Although this could be a DIY task, I would advise against this. Things could go horribly wrong. Business profits are calculated using International Financial Reporting Standards, which govern how to treat the financial transactions a business has made.

Let me give you an example of how confusing some Financial Reporting Standards have become.

What is the value of an interest-free loan of £100,000 taken out by a business and repayable five years from now (ie, the business will pay back £100,000 in five years' time)?

a) £100,000

b) £82,193

c) £116,985

Until recently, the answer was a). Now, the correct answer is b)! This is based on the present spending value of money. Assuming the cost of money on the bank loan markets is 4% each year, the value of £100,000 received in five years in today's terms is £82,193. (This represents the amount of money you would need to invest now that, with 4% per annum growth, would amount to £100,000 in five years' time.) What happens to the difference of £17,807? That goes to the business profit-and-loss account, which is taxable in that year.

Once the annual accounts are produced, you can then calculate the tax due on the profits, and also know how much is available to pay out as dividends.

Wouldn't it be better if you knew how much tax you were going to have to pay and how much you could legally draw down as you went along? That's all possible if your system is set up to automatically produce those figures for you.

Statutory matters

To balance out the protection of limited liability status, LLPs and limited companies are both required to submit accounts in a specified form to Companies House. There are a myriad of exemptions and requirements based on the size of the business. The standard submission time limit for both an LLP and a limited company is nine months after the period end (or in the case of a new start-up, twenty-one months after incorporation).

The statutory accounts have been developed with legislation in mind and are used for the following:

1. To calculate the taxable profits and subsequently the tax

2. To calculate the distributable reserves

3. To provide a basis for credit-rating agencies to apply a credit score

The accounts are *not* the most appropriate tool to manage your business on a day-to-day basis, nor are they the most appropriate method for valuing your business (see Chapter 8).

The corporation tax return is completed using the statutory accounts as the basis, but the profits can then be amended in line with specific taxable and non-taxable adjustments (eg, entertaining and depreciation of assets).

The tax for companies with annual profits of less than £1.5 million is due nine months and one day after the period end. If the period is longer than twelve months, two returns will be required.

Companies House also requires a confirmation statement every year. To complete one, simply check the business information you registered at Companies House and confirm that it's accurate and up to date. The information on public record you will have to check and confirm includes the following:

- Company name and registration number

- Registered office address

- Information about each director

- Information about each company secretary

- Principal business activities (Standard Industrial Classification codes)

- Name of each shareholder

- Shares held by each shareholder – class, quantity and details of any transfers

- Statement of capital

- Information about people with significant control (PSCs)

You are required to submit the accounts and the confirmation statement annually. In addition, you also need to prepare periodic payroll returns (quarterly, monthly, or weekly), VAT returns, and benefit-in-kind returns (P11Ds). You must also keep records of dividends paid.

Many entrepreneurs trip up over the above, or account for things incorrectly. The most common issue is not understanding the difference between a director's private funds and company funds.

Often, understandably, entrepreneurs just want to obtain results and will either use private funds (eg, personal credit cards) rather than business funds, or do the opposite and spend company funds (because they're there) on private items. If this happens, a director's loan account will be created, either an asset if funds are due to the company or a liability if they are due to the director.

To overcome this, keep an up-to-date statement of your director's loan account. Cloud accounting systems will help you create a report that will enable you to keep a running balance and also predict any problems that could arise in the future.

The most common problem arises if a director owes the company more than £10,000 and doesn't repay it within nine months. The company will then be required to pay a loan tax charge of 32.5% of the outstanding balance. If the director repays the loan within four years, the company can reclaim the loan tax charge against future corporation tax. Keeping a track of the loan account balance is therefore critical to controlling this tax.

Entrepreneurs should be spending their time working on their ideas and plans rather than on detailed compliance work. With this in mind, hire a great accountant from the beginning and see it as an investment. If you think your accountant is expensive, remember, the cost of a cheap accountant is much more in the long run!

SIX

Identify Insights

A s the leader of the business you need insights into what's happening at an early stage. You need to spot trends, identify problems, fill gaps in your product line, and generally have the information necessary to take your business to the next level.

Once your business is up and running, it takes on a life of its own. It will have its own heartbeat. The day-to-day activities will become habitual.

Most business activities have financial consequences, and because of the authorities' need to levy tax, accountants follow set formats to record results. That's all great for the tax man, but are tax compliant accounts the best form of information for the entrepreneur? I would argue they aren't.

Measure the things that matter

Almost every new client I meet (before we have worked together) measures their success by their bank balance. Why is that? Two key reasons: One, it's easy to obtain in today's digital world. Two, it's easy to understand (it's a simple figure and, to a degree, a useful measure).

The next level up is to have annual accounts (in the best format for the tax authorities rather than you). However, you need to wait a year before you know how you performed! What's better still is to have management accounts, quarterly or even monthly. These generally follow the tax authorities' formats.

When I started out in business, management accounts were the best option available. However, the world changed with the onset of cloud accounting (ie, software such as Xero and QuickBooks). I adopted cloud accounting early on, as I saw how it gave us as professional advisers the ability to fundamentally change our relationships with our clients for the better. Suddenly we were working together, on literally the same web page, with current, real-time information.

To understand the importance of looking at your business numbers, consider this. Imagine you're part of a typical UK family: two adults, two children and a dog. That's your asset base in this analogy. Now imagine one child takes the dog for a walk and disappears.

You would probably call the police and start searching for them. It would be a highly emotional situation. And quite urgent!

Now consider this: how would you feel if 25% of your business disappeared? The situation wouldn't be as emotional, but it would certainly be disastrous. If you look at your numbers only quarterly in arrears, when would you find out you'd lost this business?

At least ninety days too late!

Hopefully this analogy emphasises the need to stay up to date on your business numbers. You might say that it couldn't happen to you, but it's happened to businesses I've worked with, right under their noses, so I would argue it certainly could.

HOW TO LOSE A QUARTER OF YOUR BUSINESS FROM UNDER YOUR NOSE

A manufacturing distributor I worked with some years ago thought they were selling their product with 34% margin (ie, every £1 sold had direct costs of 66p). They had told their team to price appropriately to make 34%, and they had invested in a warehouse and factory overheads to break even at 25% margin. With 34% margin they would make £220,000 profit per annum – very healthy. But when they looked at the actual prices, costs and delivery charges, the margin was much less: only 19%. With

19% margin they were actually losing money at a rate of £230,000 per year.

What would you prefer? To know in advance that you're going to make a loss (and have the chance to take action)? Or to find out in four months that you made a loss several months ago?

So, how often do you measure your performance?

Measuring the bank balance won't give you accurate enough information to know if you've made a loss. However, even if you did know you'd made a loss, you should have been taking action to prevent the loss in the first place. That's where key predictive indicators come in.

Your bank balance can cloud your judgement and give you a false sense of safety. It can also be misleading if you don't understand your liabilities (eg, business tax or VAT due). The bank balance is also known as the lagging indicator, as it's a result of a decision made months ago and actions taken over many months. It could also be higher than expected if you've improved cash flow (see the previous chapter).

Key predictive indicators

One of the original key predictive indicators (KPIs) was a canary. In Victorian times, coal miners would take canaries down into the mines with them. If the canary stopped singing and fell off its perch, the miners knew the air quality was dangerous. This KPI measured something that really mattered: a life-or-death indicator.

The miners' emergency breathing masks had between six and thirteen minutes of air. So, when a canary fell off its perch, miners were very quick to put their breathing masks on and move themselves away from the danger zone.

The moral of the story is this: it's one thing to have a great predictor; it's another to take action, and to take action fast. To ensure your business succeeds, start measuring what matters to your customers and create KPIs. They will become your business canary.

What measures work and why

I learned at an early age that you can only help people do something if they understand the reasons why it's worth doing.

In 1994, Continental Airlines was failing badly. During the previous ten years, they had filed for bankruptcy twice. Then Gordon Bethune took the helm. He reviewed the management strategy at Continental and concluded that their main drivers should be reducing the running costs and the cost per available seat mile. Following his analysis, Bethune discarded the existing strategy. He pointed out, 'We aren't in business to save money, we are in business to put out a good product. It's the old adage: "You can make a pizza so cheap, nobody will eat it." You can make an airline so cheap, nobody will fly it.'

Continental shifted their focus away from costs and started tracking three leading KPIs:

- On-time arrival – a speed of delivery measure

- Lost luggage – a quality measure

- Customer complaints – a customer satisfaction measure

What's significant about the above measures is that they mattered to the airline's customers. Profits began to soar once the company started focusing on measures that made a dramatic difference to their customers.

Consider the following case study.

KPIS THAT WORK

Many business owners still don't measure the numbers that make a difference. By implementing systems to measure numbers that matter to their customers, my clients have had outstanding success. I worked with a company that had been in business for thirty years and was stuck in a rut.

They implemented a system of measurements based around their performance in terms of their customers, including *measures of delivery times* and *measures of parts rejections*. This had a dramatic effect on profits and increased the bottom line – from £30,000 profit per year to £700,000 profit per year over a three-year period.

My client started to focus on measures of delivery times and measures of parts rejections; both of these measures mattered to the business customers, and as a result, their bottom line increased over 1,300% in three years. This stuff really does work.

What happens when you start measuring the numbers that matter most to your customers?

You start to predict the future success of your business. When you track, measure, and, most importantly, act on the KPIs that matter to your customers, you create an enjoyable experience for them and increase your business' chances of success. Continental Airlines went from worst to first in the industry by simply focusing on the things that mattered to the customers. My client transformed their fortunes in the same way.

'Simply by making the effort to start something, you will be miles ahead of almost everyone else.'
— Gary Player

Creating a plan to use insights effectively

Most accountants are trained to analyse the standard lagging measures, such as profit-and-loss sheets and balance sheets. While these things have value, they won't help you create value for your business and your customers.

So how do you decide what aspects of your business to measure?

You need to revisit your business value proposition. We briefly covered this in 'Assess your situation'. What are you doing to create value for your customers? What's important to your customers? Then, work out ways of measuring the value you're providing. If you focus on that you will excel. Also, you're more likely to take action on measures if they're being monitored publicly.

Measuring the wrong things will lead you to focus on the wrong things, and will ultimately produce the wrong behaviours, which is why it's so important to measure the correct indicators. If my client had simply focused on cutting costs, they likely would have closed down, and their eighty employees would be out of employment, too.

Once you have identified the two or three key indicators that matter to your customers, make them

A blueprint for monitoring costs

Customer Measures

	Target	Actual	Var
Operational			
Product rejects	5%	10%	5%
On time delivery %	99%	95%	-4%
Customer feedback %	9	7	-2
Marketing			
Leads	20	25	5
Appointments	10	10	0
Proposals	7	8	1
Sales	20000	19000	-1000
No of Customers	1000	980	-20
Average Customer Spend	166.67	188.78	22.109
Frequency of Spend	4	3.5	-0.5
Customers left	5	6	1

Cost Measures

	Target	Actual	Var
Gross Profit%	25.00%	32.43%	7.43%
Gross Profit	41,667	60,000	18,333
Delivery Spend %	2.00%	2.00%	0.00%
Delivery Costs	3,333	3,700	367
Software Costs	6,000	5,467	(533)
Labour %	30%		-30%
Labour Costs	50,000	53,567	3,567

Actual v Previous Forecast / Future Forecast

	Forecast	Actual	Mth 1	Mth 2	Mth 3
Sales	166,667	185,000	180,000	183,000	195,000
Cost of Sales	125,000	125,000	135,000	137,250	146,250
Gross Profit	41,667	60,000	45,000	45,750	48,750
Overhead	16,667	16,667	16,667	16,667	16,667
EBITA(2)	25,000	43,333	28,333	29,083	32,083
Depreciation	4,167	4,167	4,167	4,167	4,167
Tax	4,750	8,233	5,383	5,526	6,096
Net Profit	16,083	30,933	18,783	19,391	21,821
Dividends (1)	5,000	5,000	5,001	5,002	5,003
Cash in Bank	50,000	25,000	55,000	60,000	65,000
Business Value	1,800,000	3,120,000	2,040,000	2,094,000	2,310,000

Appropriate highlights eg rent rise

public and celebrate improvements in those numbers. Remember, choose only a few; otherwise, they won't be key. Initially, you'll likely need to put in measurement systems to give you the numbers. These key indicators may not have been measured before: in our example, on-time delivery percentage may not have been measured systematically, so you will need to devise a system to measure it. It's as simple as recording the number of deliveries sent and the number arriving on time. If possible, don't reinvent the wheel – you may be able to pull in measurements from existing reports. Only create new systems for key indicators.

Of course, you will still need to monitor costs, but that should be relatively easy, as shown in this simple blueprint.

This blueprint could serve as a base for your information. Depending on your business, you'll need to tailor it for your KPIs to give you a deeper understanding of your business and help your decision making.

Many modern entrepreneurs conduct sales via web shops such as Shopify or WooCommerce. Used correctly, these platforms can provide valuable insight into what works and what doesn't in terms of marketing initiatives.

We regularly provide in-depth customer insights to our clients. For example, if you have two complementary products and you know a customer has bought one but not the other, wouldn't it be wise to market the other product to that customer? Paying attention to details like this shows you care about the customer, and it also increases your profits!

When measuring performance, you need to keep each business division separate. Often this division is geographical. If you look only at the company as a whole, it's easy to miss certain facts (eg, one unit is profitable and the other makes a loss).

KEEP ON TOP OF EACH DIVISION

Insights into your business enable decisions to be made. A client that specialised in food labelling, and operated around the globe, had several divisions. The group as a whole was profitable, but then one of its divisions underwent a dramatic change of fortune. It lost some key personnel while at the same time increasing its office space. They lost customers and had higher costs. By keeping a close eye on that division, they were able to take the decision to stop losing six figures in that area by closing the division and servicing some of the remaining customers from other parts of the global business.

By monitoring what matters, you can make key decisions quickly and decisively.

Once you have your reporting systems in place to give you the necessary decision-making information, you can move ahead and start enhancing your business.

SEVEN

Enhance The Business

Running an entrepreneurial business involves taking many factors into account. At both a macro level and a company level, things are always changing: legislation, fashion, technology, communication methods – the list goes on. What is clear is that you can't stand still. To use an old phrase, 'Today's news is tomorrow's fish and chip wrapping.' Even that phrase is out of date; news is mostly online now, and food hygiene rules won't allow newspapers as food packaging!

The pace of change accelerates every year. The table below outlines the world's most valuable companies in 2017.

Forbes top companies in the world by market value in 2017

	Market value in US$bn	Annual growth rate in US$bn
Apple	752.0	35.8
Alphabet (Google)	579.5	29.0
Microsoft	507.5	11.8
Amazon.com	427.0	17.8

Apple almost went out of business in 1997, Alphabet (Google) didn't start until 1998, Microsoft started in 1975 and Amazon started in 1994. They all went from nothing to the top in a very short space of time. To highlight the annual growth I have simply divided the market value by the years since inception (for Apple, it's since it almost closed). You can see that they have grown at a phenomenal annual rate, the lowest (Microsoft) increasing by almost $1bn ($11.8bn/12) each and every month (using a simple average).

Newcomers such as Facebook, Snapchat and the like are accelerating even faster. What do they have in common? They redefine markets.

Apple has redefined phones and created completely new product and service categories (personal music devices, tablets). Google has redefined the advertising world. Microsoft introduced personal computing, and Amazon has redefined shopping.

A successful business does not stand still

You need to look at your business and make sure it's leading the market rather than following it. Recent history is full of businesses that didn't change fast enough:

- Yellow Pages (will cease to be printed after 2019 – online only)
- Blockbuster Video (closed in the UK 2013)
- Motorola (split and sold to Lenovo and Google)
- Sears (hasn't traded profitably since 2010)
- Sun Microsystems
- Toys 'R' Us

None are the leaders they once were, and some are out of business. In essence, they lost touch with their customers and failed to produce value for them. It's critical to understand that overall value is what's most important to your customer – not price.

Blockbuster rented out movies but was usurped by Netflix, which also rents out movies but uses a different delivery mechanism and method of pricing. Blockbuster arguably should have seen it coming. Motorola was dominant in the phone handset market when there was a trend toward smaller and smaller phones. Today, the consumer wants a phone with fundamentally more communication options (eg, an iPhone).

Technology is changing markets, so virtually all sectors need to adapt and utilise technology in the most appropriate way or suffer the consequences. You need to consider how you can embrace technology to improve your business proposition or, indeed, reinvent your business proposition. I will repeat it for emphasis:

A successful business does not stand still! To move forward, you should regularly review the following key areas.

Marketing

Marketing is what generates the base for future sales, and it flows through almost all functions of a business to some degree. Customers – past, present and future – all come to your business to fulfil a need. You need to educate them constantly about the value you create to ensure you have a demand at the maximum price possible. You need to remember that your marketing must be congruent with your brand, and this congruence will be what shapes the demand. Porsche marketing leads to much higher prices than Dacia (the UK's cheapest new car).

To grow, all businesses must do four things:

1. Increase customer numbers – this is usually the key focus of most businesses

2. Sell to customers more often – much less focus is given to this

3. Increase the average spend of each customer – not enough businesses measure this

4. Reduce the customer defection rate – monitoring this can produce many insights

Customers don't wake up and suddenly want to buy your product or service. At some point in the past, they were persuaded that they needed it. And that persuasion usually comes down to emotion rather than the product or service itself. The customer has a perceived idea of how he or she will feel after making the purchase.

The emotions of all buyers (both consumer and businesses) fall into the following categories:

- **A desire to save time:** At a basic level, people want time to make more of their lives

- **A desire to avoid pain:** This is much more common than conventional wisdom predicts; it's about reducing risk (eg, experiencing peace of mind, complying with laws, having basic necessities)

- **A desire to feel pleasure:** This may be direct, eg, feelings of happiness or euphoria or, more commonly, indirect, eg, in a business context, a product or service that will enable your company to succeed is likely to generate a feeling of pleasure

What emotional need does your product or service meet, and why? Once you know this, you can harness your marketing efforts to creating a product/service designed with the buyers' desires in mind, which will increase demand.

The next step is to target the appropriate buyers. You need to work out who they are so you can find out where they are.

Finally, you can employ technology to help you create and deliver the messages that drive buyers to your market, for example, targeted messages through Facebook, Google and Instagram.

Packaging your offering

Now that you understand your customers, you can package your offering to appeal to them. The most successful businesses do this extremely well.

Consider the following.

Q. When you need a plumber, what are the things that you worry about?

A. Will they turn up on time?

A. Will they tidy up after themselves?

A. Will they rip me off?

If you found a plumber that was on time, tidy and fair, you would stick with them, and you would recommend them to your friends, family and colleagues too. Conversely, if you found a plumber that was late, messy and ripped you off, you wouldn't use them again and you wouldn't recommend them – and you might even go as far as telling your family and friends to avoid them.

Q. What frustrates people about eating out locally?

A. Waiting ages for the food to arrive

A. The menu item they want is unavailable

A. Dirty toilets

A. Lack of parking

What could the restaurant do to address these frustrations?

- Offer a waiting time guarantee and deliver on it

- Have a simplified menu with all dishes always available

- Refurbish the toilets

- Suggest parking spaces and refund parking charges

If a business addresses common frustrations and delivers on its promises *each and every time*, it will win more customers and begin to build brand value.

The entrepreneur's value is in their ability to develop the solution and then systematise it, so it can be implemented every time.

Pricing

Pricing is a huge topic. It's an art not a science, and the art of pricing could be an entire book in itself, but I've outlined a few important points to always bear in mind.

Essentially, there are two types of pricing: cost plus and value based.

Cost-plus pricing has been around for ages. This is by far the easiest way to price and is common in the services industries. The manufacturer or service provider works out how much it costs to create the product or service and factors in profit margin to create the price. Hourly-rate pricing is also a form of cost-plus pricing. In this case, profit must be estimated. Solicitors often use this method. Widget manufacturers and retail businesses often use a variation of this, in that they work out the costs per unit, taking into account all the costs to produce the goods, then add a profit margin.

But in the twentieth century, economists researched various forms of pricing and concluded that value pricing is the way to achieve optimum results. The *Financial Times* lexicon provides a great definition of value pricing:

> 'The term is used when prices are based on the value of the product as perceived from the customer's perspective. The perceived value determines the customer's willingness to pay and thus the maximum price the company can charge for its product.'

Once you have your core value offer you need to price it. As I've said throughout this book, all buyers want value:

Perceived customer = the total positive benefit
value   less the price paid

Often sellers get hung up on price, but if they have the right customer, they should be concerned about value.

The profit-building power of pricing

The following example highlights the potential power of effective pricing. Say you're an entrepreneurial retailer (with online and wholesale customers) and offer a range of products. Your total sales are £1,250,000 per annum.

The cost of those sales is £775,000, with an overall gross margin of £475,000 (38%). After salaries and overheads, the business' net profit is £90,000 (7.2%).

The 'What if?' reckoner

Annual turnover	£ 1,250,000
Gross margin	38%
Annual cost of production/sales	£ 775,000
Annual cost of overheads	£ 385,000
Profit for the year	£ 90,000

If you increase the average price of sales by 1% across all the business income sources with no other changes, the effect on the net profit 'bottom line' is an increase from £90,000 to £102,500 (£12,500 or 13.8%). This is significantly more than most owners would expect.

What if you increase the price by 10%? The net profit jumps by a whopping 139%. It's not some conjuring trick – it's the maths. And when you increase your net profit, you also increase the valuation of your business (see Chapter 8), as net profit forms a basis for most valuations.

But so many businesses worry about the competition and being price competitive that they do the opposite:

they reduce prices to sell more, and their profits fall drastically. You might think a 10% price increase will mean all your customers go elsewhere. It's possible, but what are the numbers? In this case, you could lose 26% of your customers and have the same net profits as before. And those that do leave are probably the ones you least want to keep anyway.

The 'What if?' results

	Before	With 10% price rise	10% price rise losing 26% of customers
Annual turnover	£ 1,250,000	£ 1,375,000	£ 1,046,053
Gross margin	38%	44%	44%
Annual cost of production/sales	£ 775,000	£ 775,000	£ 571,053
Annual cost of overheads	£ 385,000	£ 385,000	£ 385,000
Profit for the year	£ 90,000	£ 215,000	£ 90,000

I'm not suggesting you just ramp up prices. The reason I use these numbers is to help you realise the massive importance pricing has in your marketing efforts. Far too many people only focus on turnover and, in doing so, sell their product or services for a cheaper and cheaper price, to hit targets. This reduces the average price, which ultimately leads to lower profits. It's a bit like running faster on a treadmill that's also speeding up.

Why value pricing?

Value pricing looks at the price from the customer's perspective rather than the producer's perspective. It's far more customer friendly and will usually result in much higher profits for the business providing the product or service.

Here's an example of value pricing in action. A major logistics distribution company relied heavily on their IT infrastructure. Their profits were in the millions. On one occasion, their IT system failed. Every lost minute meant lost orders and lost profits, as well as delays for their customers. They stood to lose £1 million for every lost day. The company tried to repair the situation in house but failed and had to call in an engineer. The engineer came along, went straight to a particular server, flicked a switch and brought back the system.

He produced a bill of £10,000. The managing director of the logistics company questioned the size of the bill, as the engineer had spent only an hour on site (and most of this time was spent negotiating with security, trying to get into the building), and asked for an itemised bill. The engineer produced this bill, which had two lines on it. Line one: £100 for time to flick switch. Line two: £9,900 for knowing which switch to flick. The managing director approved the bill without further questions.

The point is that to obtain the maximum value of our product or service, we need to ensure that our customers are fully aware of the value to them.

Optimal pricing

Value pricing is tough because value is subjective and therefore difficult to put a number on. We all value things differently. That's why it's important to have a system that allows price discrimination, effectively selling the same product to different groups at different prices. A classic example is peak and off-peak travel: the same journey at different prices at different times of the day. Your system should help you tap into the psychology of your customers, so as to maximise their value perception and willingness to pay.

The ultimate form of value pricing is optimal pricing. This means setting your prices at the maximum each individual customer is willing to pay – in other words, that particular customer's optimal price.

Retailers are now much more aware of the psychology of pricing and have multiple ways of obtaining the optimal price. For example, say you want to buy a 75-inch LED TV and your budget is £2000. If you visit a major electronics store, you'll be immediately struck with a vast array of options. The store will likely have a number of models that are within your budget and some a little outside of it. It's their job to maximise the amount that you spend. Similar TVs will be displayed close together, and some will have slightly better features than others. It's therefore easy for you to compare models and think, 'I'd like that extra little feature, or that function.' Rather than look at the overall prices, you look at the differences between the models. You're only making a decision on a small amount and are therefore much more likely to say yes to a TV not within your budget.

Web stores use the same methods. You might visit Apple's website to look at a MacBook Air and end up purchasing a MacBook Pro, which is more expensive. The store is set up to help you make decisions based on relatively small price increments.

Why does this work?

It's human nature to compare things. We tend to find estimating the absolute value of something much more difficult than comparing two things. We need a point of reference to be able to work out a measurement.

For instance, look at the room around you now. Could you tell me the area of it? Unless you have some prior knowledge or are an architect, probably not. However, if you looked at the adjacent room and I told you it was 60 m², you could easily tell me whether the room you're in is larger or smaller than this. It's simply the way our brains work.

Using human nature to your advantage

First of all, forget about how much something costs to make or how long it takes to produce. Both these figures are irrelevant to the customer. (Of course, for internal purposes, you need to make sure that your prices are higher than your costs. If they aren't, you might as well do something else.)

Now consider this. A relatively new branch of economics, called behavioural economics, reveals that in many cases, buying decisions aren't rational.

The human brain can make extremely complex calculations and move rapidly in ways that even the most powerful artificial-intelligence-based computers can't compete with. Take the simple act of catching a ball. Think of the thousands of brain calculations that make it happen.

- Ears hear someone shout 'catch!' and attention is then captured

- Eyes find the ball (establishing an anchor point), and legs and arms instantaneously move into position; eyes keep following the trajectory of the ball, and hands grasp the ball at the appropriate time – the ball's location throughout the process has been continuously compared to the initial anchor point

The brain processes so much information in such a small space of time, yet the act of catching the ball seems trivial, even for young children.

Despite its incredible abilities, the brain can also be easily fooled. In 2006, Drazen Prelec and Dan Ariely conducted a study at MIT in which they had students bid on items in a bizarre auction. In his book *Predictably Irrational*, Ariely explains that the researchers would hold up a bottle of wine, or a textbook or a cordless trackball and then describe in detail how awesome the item was. Then each student had to write down the last two digits of their social security number. This number would become the price of the item; if the last two digits were 11, then the item was priced at $11. After they wrote down the pretend price, they bid. Sure enough, the anchoring effect scrambled their ability to judge the value of the items. People with high social security numbers paid up to 346% more for an item than those with low numbers. People with numbers from 80 to 99 paid, on average, $26 for the item, while those with 00 to 19 paid around $9.

The brains of students at one of the most prestigious educational institutions in the world were easily fooled.

There are similarities between the ball-catching exercise and the auction. Importantly, in both examples there was an anchor – as Dan Ariely explains: 'Social security numbers were the anchor in the MIT experiment only because they were easy to use and obviously random. The researchers could have just as well asked for the current temperature or the manufacturer's suggested retail price.'

Most buying decisions are made using two basic human abilities: the ability to anchor and the ability to compare. Once you're aware of this, you can use it to help your customers make purchasing decisions.

Setting the anchor

The most important part of the process is setting the anchor. If you set the anchor incorrectly, you will struggle to move prices very far from that point. Setting the anchor is all about helping customers understand where the start point is. If your service is easily categorised and comparable to something already commonly available, your anchor has been set for you. If you create a category, as Apple did with iPads, you can create your own anchor and effectively control the market.

If the product category already exists, then branding and packaging helps to set the anchor. Everything else is relative. Apple's latest phone, the iPhone X, has struggled to break through the $1,000 barrier in the US because Apple set its anchor point at $700–$800 with earlier iPhones. The latest models are simply not different enough in customers' minds to need a new anchor. Although the product is by no means a failure, the sales numbers haven't reached original expectations.

Successful brands set anchors using congruent branding messages. You can do the same in your business. If you're in a high-quality market, you need to set your anchor appropriately high.

Here's an extreme example. How much would you pay for a bottle of water? There's one that has a price tag of $60,000 for 750 ml. This is how it's described:

> 'This glass bottle of water is encased in 24k gold and features a sculpture based on artwork by the late Italian artist, Amedeo Clemente Modigliani.
>
> The contents of the bottle hold a mixture of natural spring water from France, Fiji and glacial water from Iceland. Mixed into the water is also 5mg of gold dust.
>
> The designer, creator and owner of this rare bottle of water – Paolo di Verachi, also won the Guinness World Record for the most expensive bottle of water.'

It's not even pure!

Yes, it's extreme, but it shows the importance of the anchoring and positioning of the product. You can anchor and position the price with any product or service, but making that happen requires planning and consistency.

First of all you need to work out what the customer values, and this will be different in different industries. If you're in a service industry or in retail, you need to give the customer the ability to make comparisons with things that they value.

The simplest example of giving a customer value is to save them money. If you save them £100, then you have given value of £100. In theory, you can charge the customer anything up to £100. But if they don't know you saved them £100, how can you justify charging them anything?

The key is to identify the value to your customer and use it as a basis for setting your price. In my experience, too little time is spent on this. What commonly happens is that businesses look at what their competition is charging and then charge a little bit less. This is categorically the wrong way to price.

Instead, you should ask questions of your customers to establish what is important to them. Depending on your industry, the form the questions take will differ. At one extreme, the questions could take the form of a well-structured shop which leads customers to their optimal price. At the other extreme, you might ask them questions directly, face to face. Generally, the higher the value of the product or service, the more questions need to be asked.

In today's technological world, we can manage the pricing process intelligently. A simple but modern example of establishing the value is common with car servicing. The process is as follows.

Stage One: Inspect the car to assess its faults and service needs. At this point, the mechanic will identify what needs to be done. The customer is still unaware of any problem. How can the problem be conveyed to the customer? An easy option is to create a video of the inspection, while the car is in the service bay. Safety issues can be highlighted and categorised, and shown to the customer with some scripted commentary.

Stage Two: Present the video to the customer online and link it to a shopping basket of specific repair items that the customer can select.

Stage Three: Categorise the repair items as:

a) A safety issue

b) Recommended to be fixed within three months

c) Needs attention before the next service

Stage Four: The customer selects the repairs they wish to have done and enters their card details to pay for the transaction.

The above process could be used in many different situations. The key point is that it's customer-centric. It demonstrates the value to the customer and enables them to make informed decisions.

Using such a system will enable you to charge more and, importantly, will allow the customer to buy from you at a price which is ideal for them. It's not absolutely perfect but close, and it certainly achieves greater customer buying potential than the mechanic simply taking a deep breath and plucking a figure from his or her head.

There are no hard and fast rules for pricing, but as long as you make a profit, cost should not be a factor.

There is no such thing as the right price

Unless you can read minds, you have no idea how much customers are willing and able to spend. Even if you could read minds, it wouldn't help much because usually the customers don't know either! How many times, when you are the customer, have you spent more than you thought you would in a shop?

The process of determining the optimal price is more important than the actual numbers. Should you increase the price by 20% or 30% if a customer wants a certain function? There is absolutely no way of knowing that until you begin to test.

As a general rule, price high and then build in enough options and upgrades to allow your customers to get to the price point where they say yes or you decide they're not the right customers for you.

Products and branding

Products and the branding of these products make what you do more tangible – and this helps create value and improve profitability. A well-known brand imparts its value to everything it's attached to.

For example, Nike's logo is a simple shape, but once it's added to a piece of clothing, the price of the item increases. Two virtually identical pairs of trainers could range in price from £20 to £100, based on a logo. Multiply that by the number of trainers sold and the value of a brand is clearly in the multimillions.

As an entrepreneur, you need to have a brand that encapsulates your ethos and values from the start and stick to it on your business journey. Once you define your brand you should commission a branding document, to ensure all future marketing will be congruent with your business.

Productisation

Productisation is the process of packaging a service, solution or product with a specific name so that it can be presented as a product.

To build value and enhance profits, it's crucial that you productise everything you sell and do. This is applicable to both goods and services.

Countless examples of productisation exist in the UK economy. For example, Mercedes has several classes (A, B, C, E, S) and BMW has several series (1, 2, 3, 4, 5). Product names enable customers to visualise exactly what's on offer. They also give them the opportunity to buy at their price points; as we saw previously, there is no such thing as the right price. British Gas productises its range of HomeCare items, which are actually services bundled into products. They have HomeCare One to HomeCare Four, each of which comprises a different range of services and there is a corresponding range of prices from which the customer can choose.

Around 80% of UK GDP is now based on some form of service, so most entrepreneurs will need to master productisation.

In today's business economy, it's imperative that entrepreneurs understand their customers' motives. It's also a significant competitive advantage to understand how your customers create value for their customers and how you fit into that. You can then ensure your offerings complement theirs.

By mastering the art of productisation, you will create value for your intangible assets and help ensure consistent delivery to your customers. The advantages of productisation are numerous.

- Efficiency, profitability and competitiveness are increased (a productised service is repeatable)

- The item becomes a scalable asset (which can be sold many more times than something that isn't productised)

- Service delivery is less time consuming because the methods and processes have been thought through

- An expert's time can become an information package. This package can be flexibly created from suitable modular elements of the overall service. You can then create a customised service, which is a collection of standard productised services (similar to customising a car with particular extras)

- A key point of differentiation from competitors is created; a named productised service enhances the credibility of what you do

- It's easier to market something that is standardised

- The customer knows what they're buying, and the provider knows what they're selling

- A packaged service becomes independent of any one individual, which reduces reliance and risk for the business; if all the knowledge is in one individual's head and this individual leaves, the knowledge leaves with them – it's not an asset of the business

- It allows the entrepreneur to step away from the day-to-day tasks of the business: the entrepreneur can work *on* the business, not *in* the business

Of course, productisation is not possible for every service. To productise a service, the service must be of real customer value (ie, it should address a genuine customer need *and* create value for the customer). The service must also recur reasonably frequently. It's ideal for complex services.

An entrepreneurial business generally has an advantage over large established businesses due to its agility and ability to change. Changing the culture of executive management boards with significant bureaucratic hurdles to overcome is a difficult and relatively slow task. And individuals within larger corporations tend to hold on to knowledge, as they perceive knowledge to equate to status. Consequently, they will be reluctant to productise their knowledge.

Though productisation offers many benefits, it also presents several practical hurdles that need to be overcome.

- Any new idea will meet resistance. People are generally reluctant to change, but consider one of the basic laws of nature, which is that it's not the most intellectual, or the strongest, species that survives, but the one that is best able to adapt and adjust to the changing environment in which it finds itself. The same applies to entrepreneurial businesses.

- It's hard work to recreate process techniques and, as a result, to productise services, so easier simple tasks take precedence.

- Smaller entrepreneurial businesses lack the know-how to productise or the resources to outsource the function.

- There is a general fear that once something is productised, competitors will copy the idea. (The reality is that the service processes will be too complex to imitate. It's actually an opportunity to create value. Also, the product can be formally registered as intellectual property.)

- Services are usually developed in real time in conjunction with customers, employees and technology. Recreating a process which is the sum of several moving parts is challenging.

Despite all the above, though, the gains of productisation in terms of customer experience far outweigh the challenges:

Customer experience = The internal and
subjective response
customers have to any
direct or indirect contact
with a business

In essence, customer experience is the sum of all contact a customer has with a business. All parts of the business should focus on providing an integrated, memorable and favourable customer experience that wows each and every customer.

The sum of all your customers' experiences contributes to quality, value, and, ultimately, the brand. It's what makes your business a success, and it can result in significant profits. Think of quality brands: it's not just about the actual item. If you buy an iPhone, for instance, all the touchpoints throughout the buying experience contribute to the brand: the advertising, the stores (web or physical), the retail store team, the boxes the products are shipped in, and finally the quality of the product – all of these play their part.

With the benefits of repeatable top-quality service throughout the organisation now clear, you need a method to make this happen for your business.

Achieving productisation in your business

The first step is to create a service blueprint. A service blueprint is customer focused and allows businesses to present their service processes graphically. It incorporates points of customer contact and the physical evidence (eg, booking form, web form, etc) associated with the service from the customer's viewpoint.

Once the service components are mapped out, you can identify which underlying support services will help to create a complete and focused customer experience.

A typical service blueprint has five components.

1. Physical evidence

2. Customer actions

3. Visible (to the customer) business action
_____ line of interaction _____

4. Invisible (to the customer) business actions

5. Support processes

It's worth mentioning again: a service blueprint is customer-centric. So, the customers' actions come first. Next are the visible business actions, followed by the line of interaction, that is, the line between what is visible to the customer and what isn't. All interactions above this line are chances to wow the customer.

Below the line of interaction is all the back-office stuff that makes the customer-visible stuff possible.

The table below is simple overview of a service blueprint for a golf pay-and-play centre.

Service blueprint mapping

Physical evidence	An order form/ web page	Receptionist's uniform and welcome script	History of scores visible on bay screen
Customer actions	Complete the form and make the booking	Arrive at the centre	Go to nominated bay
Visible (to the customer) business actions		Greet the customer and give them equipment	Explain latest updates/ weekly targets to customer
Invisible (to the customer) business actions	Process the booking – reserve the equipment		Transfer equipment to correct bay
Support processes	Equipment preparation system (cleaning and repair)	Registration system (list of expected visitors)	Loading of customers' scores on bay computer

The whole process for any given service needs to be mapped out, initially as an overview and then down to the detail. The table above is just an overview. In a complete service blueprint, the table would extend as time passes.

A service blueprint helps you to map out the best possible customer experience and, importantly, to ensure it happens time and time again.

You can use the blueprint creation process to brainstorm, perhaps with your team. This process allows for blue-sky thinking but is grounded in the reality of ensuring repeatability and scalability.

You may feel overwhelmed once you start thinking about your own systems. The best way to deal with it is to break the customer process map down into smaller chunks and work through these chunks one at a time. As you do so, always remember the massive benefits productisation will produce: improved customer service, profitability and business value.

Automation

Like productisation, automation is key to enhancing the value of your business. If a process is automated, you don't have to rely on a human for it. For example, take online shopping. The customer visits a website, chooses an item and then pays for it. No human interaction occurs during the purchasing process. Of course, human interaction is needed during the website design process. Indeed, there is much more demand for sales psychology now than ever before. Behavioural economics play a big part in guiding customers subconsciously through the buying journey.

Automation, both visible and invisible, is integral in our world today, from biometric passports, online tax returns, and automated supermarket checkout tills to behind-the-scenes warehouse management systems that keep track of thousands of items per minute.

Automation makes processes repeatable and error free (as long as the processes are correctly planned). Once automated, they can then be scaled.

Use the service blueprint with your service/product to ensure all your visible actions are congruent with the anchor you're aiming to set.

Make your product unique

If your service or product is unique and has value and demand, you can set your price. Uniqueness builds loyalty (ie, repeat customers), which increases your asset value and ultimately your business value.

To make something unique, you need to specialise. All of our most successful entrepreneurs have specialised.

NICHING WORKS

One of our clients is an entrepreneur in the cosmetic industry. They have focused on one specific area within the industry and become a global expert in that field – they educate and train other small businesses across the world. In a field of intense competition, out client has ensured they are the leading expert.

Rather than focus on a spectrum of products and services, they focus on one point in the spectrum and ensure they know absolutely everything about it. And because they're leaders in the field, they can charge higher prices. People seek them out.

If they were competing in the general cosmetic market, they would need huge resources to fight the large, well-known brands (eg, Olay, Avon, L'Oréal).

We help them by providing insights that allow them to go even deeper into their markets, so that they can understand and adapt to them and keep developing what their customers need. We also help them focus on ensuring their intangible business assets are maximised, to harness the value they generate.

Think about high-quality works of art. They are unique, there is large demand for them, and the prices are out of this world. The most expensive painting ever purchased – a painting of Christ as Salvator Mundi, by Leonardo da Vinci – sold for $450 million.

That's an extreme, but if you can develop unique products or service processes around your value proposition, you will limit the amount of supply that competitors can compete with.

Sometimes niching can be a problem if the entire market fails, so you need those early key predictive indicators discussed earlier in Chapter 6.

OVER-RELIANCE ON ONE PRODUCT

Although niching is great from a marketing point of view, it can go wrong if the market you're in goes sour. You should always be reviewing the bigger picture.

One of our clients grew very quickly selling, primarily, cut flowers to the UK's petrol stations. They were featured in *The Sunday Times* Fast Track 100 as a fast-growing business. They didn't quite have a monopoly, but they were certainly the dominant player in the market. The client sourced all the cut flowers from markets in Holland. They were essentially providing a distribution service. Because of the nature of the product, they also operated on a sale-or-return basis.

One year, there was a petrol strike in the UK, and my client's business was hit hard. Their customers were petrol station customers, and since the petrol stations were closed, there were no customers. Also, as a result of the strike, petrol prices were inflated, and petrol was one of the client's significant costs. Finally, the pound's value against the euro was hit, so the cost of flowers went up.

After five years of fantastic growth, economic factors outside of our client's control meant they had to close down.

Research and development

The UK government recognises the value of uniqueness and encourages research and development to innovate and break new ground.

Entrepreneurs must be able to innovate and adapt. The UK government agrees with this philosophy and offers generous tax incentives for businesses that engage in research and development (R&D) activity. (See www.gov.uk/guidance/corporation-tax-research-and-development-rd-relief for the rules governing tax relief on R&D.)

When you think of R&D, scientific laboratories or specific specialist departments might come to mind, but it doesn't have to be as distinct as that.

In the last couple of years, I have encountered R&D activity ranging from specialist tweezers for the cosmetic industry to weapons manufacture, energy processing system development and an artificial intelligence system for use in recruitment. Quite a wide range. The key is that the process or product must be new and developed by the business. Most entrepreneurs will have an element of R&D within their business for which tax incentives could and should be claimed.

With this government tax incentive, your expenditure attributed to R&D is multiplied by 2.3, and this can then be set against your corporate tax profits.

To illustrate:

A company that pays 19% corporate tax and spends £100,000 on all the components of R&D (materials, wages, a proportion of overhead) can obtain a 130% uplift, which means they would receive £24,700 (19% × £130,000) as a tax credit or repayment from HMRC.

The UK government defines what is classified as R&D, and a summary of this definition is provided at www.gov.uk/guidance/corporation-tax-research-and-development-rd-relief

If you can extend your R&D expenditure to registering patents and trademarks, you're helping to set yourself apart and reduce the number of your competitors.

This ultimately allows you to obtain higher prices for your goods or services.

Team

Entrepreneurs are usually big-picture thinkers, but they also need a team to build their business around. It's unusual for an entrepreneur to succeed without a great team.

The perfect team will have complementary skills that come together to create a business that's more than the sum of its parts.

1+1+1+1= 5

What kind of people do you need?

I have employed many different people over the years, and far and away the most important quality in a team is attitude. You need a team that has a can-do attitude rather than a resistance attitude. What people lack in skills can usually be trained, but attitude is much more difficult to change.

Many online tools exist to help you recruit based on attitude.

It sounds obvious, but many, many entrepreneurs recruit based on skills, qualifications and experience.

After all, it's how we've been programmed since our schooldays.

A team should consist of at least the following people.

1. Entrepreneur – the ideas person who drives things forward

2. Salesperson – the person responsible for making sales, pricing and marketing

3. Operations – the person responsible for systematising the business and creating value

4. Finance – the person who keeps the score

In my experience, most entrepreneurs are decent, fair people who want to reward their teams for their efforts to help the business grow. However, across the economy as a whole, there are employers who seek to take advantage of their workforce.

Today's employment laws tend to be written to deal with the unscrupulous employer rather than the majority. Specifically, in the UK there are rules governing the following:

- The time in which a business must give written particulars to the team

- Minimum wage

- Auto enrolment

- Working hours

- Holiday time

- How disciplinary action should be taken

- How people should bring up grievances

- Equality issues
  - Gender
  - Maternity and paternity
  - Adoption
  - Racism
  - Religious beliefs
  - Disability
  - Ageism

Now consider that there is no longer a defined retirement age. There's also a raft of health and safety legislation regarding employees.

In my opinion, the balance has shifted too far in favour of the employee. Consider this simple fact. An employee may decide to leave a business and give the agreed notice (typically one month), but an employer has no similar right to sever the contract with a notice period. Additionally, HMRC charges a tax on employment (employer's national insurance, 13.8%), and employing team members can be a costly exercise.

All of the above emphasises the point that your team members are 'volunteers' and can effectively leave at any time. This is a reality check – ensure you hire the correct people and take the hiring process seriously. Remember, *hire first for attitude and then for aptitude.* You should also be looking to build a balanced team with a mix of skills. To use a football analogy, it's no good having a team of just centre-forwards or goalkeepers.

You have a limited time to make your project a success. You simply cannot afford to carry passengers on your team, so rid yourself of the bad attitudes as soon as you're able. You should engage an HR team (in house or outsourced), to ensure you stay on the correct side of constantly updated employment legislation.

HR DIY is dangerous

I had a client who thought he could cope with HR policies without any specialist support. When his business lost a major customer, he decided to downsize. In the process of downsizing, he made two women redundant, one of whom happened to be on maternity leave at the time.

The client hadn't consulted enough with the woman on maternity leave, and the employment tribunal awarded her a year's salary as compensation.

This chapter focuses on continual enhancement and improvement of your business to help it grow and increase in value, and I'll give the last word to Benjamin Franklin:

'Without continual growth and progress, such words as improvement, achievement and success have no meaning.'

EIGHT

Build Value

For many entrepreneurs, their business is one of their most significant assets; often, it's their pension fund. Over-reliance on one asset for pension provision is not the subject of this book, but the fact is, many entrepreneurs are heavily, if not exclusively, reliant on their business to provide the funds for retirement. But many don't think about building value until it's too late.

You need to start early!

Future value

To understand how businesses are valued you first need to understand how the future value of anything is assessed. This is similar to the accounting rules outlined in the section 'Staying ahead of the legislation'.

Take a simple example of a single amount of money: £1,000. How much would you pay to receive it today?

It's not a trick question – the answer is £1,000. But what if you were to receive it in a year's time? This introduces a 'cost of money' factor: you could borrow some money now, knowing that you could repay it with the £1,000 in a year's time. If the guaranteed interest rate was 4% you could borrow £961.54.

The cost of money

Number of years	Interest rate 4%	Interest rate 10%	Interest rate 15%
immediate	1,000.00	1,000.00	1,000.00
1	961.54	909.09	869.57
2	924.56	826.45	756.14
3	889.00	751.31	657.52
4	854.80	683.01	571.75
5	821.93	620.92	497.18
6	790.31	564.47	432.33
7	759.92	513.16	375.94
8	730.69	466.51	326.90
9	702.59	424.10	284.26
10	675.56	385.54	247.18

The table above shows how much you would receive – with 100% certainty assuming interest rates stayed at 4% – if you extended that approach over the next ten years. It's hypothetical but bear with me. I have given amounts for the value in the future with interest rates of 10% and 15%.

The table highlights how the future value of £1,000 can change depending on when you receive it and the interest rate. That is the easy bit, as you can calculate it precisely.

Now imagine the interest rates are risk indicators – in many ways they are a measure of risk. Now consider that our £1,000 represent the profits from a business: how much would you pay for it if it was coming from a low-risk, medium-risk or high-risk business at a future point in time.

Valuing a business follows that rationale; it's a balance of future risk and return.

Determining the value of your business

Ultimately, what a business is worth is what someone else is willing to pay for it. How is that value calculated? An investor will pay an amount that fairly (in their opinion) represents the returns they are likely to obtain in the future, taking into account a risk-adjusting factor.

In simple terms, it boils down to this:

Valuation = *future* adjusted net profits (X) × the
risk multiple (Y)

Let's break this down further. X is the future (not the past) adjusted net profits, otherwise known as future maintainable earnings (usually earnings before interest, tax, depreciation and amortisation). It's a bit of a mouthful, but that's the terminology used by many legal professionals to try to confuse entrepreneurs.

Y, 'the risk multiple', is the factor by which your adjusted profits are multiplied to give you the valuation measure. It's an important number, as it *amplifies many times* all the effort you have put into creating a profitable business. Y tends to be overlooked until it's too late, but it should be managed from Day 1. This is how the clever people make serious money.

Factors affecting X

Future maintainable earnings need to be predicted in light of possible changes to the business. Valuers will look at the earnings potential and factor in the following:

1. **Systems** – This can't be emphasised enough: if a business has strong, comprehensive systems (meaning future income is not dependent on individual personnel) then there will be much less risk in terms of future earnings.

2. **Over-reliance on a few customers or suppliers** – If the business deals with only a few customers, this will increase the risk to future income. What if one goes bust? Or leaves?

3. **Future macroeconomic changes** – Macroeconomic factors outside the business' control can lead to problems (see the case study 'Over-reliance on one product'.) If a business is in an area dependent, for example, on low fuel prices, such as distribution, there could be a perception that fuel costs will rise in future and reduce future earnings.

4. **Known future events** – If changes can be predicted with any certainty, ie due to a written agreement or contract, they will be factored in. It's common for verbal agreements to be put in place but never documented (eg, a sales incentive scheme between the business and entities that refer new business to it).

This list isn't meant to be exhaustive, but should provide an idea of the typical issues that arise.

Factors affecting the Y multiplier

The table below outlines the various factors that can have an impact on Y.

Key factors affecting Y

Factor	Increases multiplier	Decreases multiplier
1. Risk	Lower	Higher
2. Systems	Comprehensive	None
3. Designs	Registered	None
4. Trademarks	Registered	None
5. Recurring income	More	Less
6. Patents	Registered	None
7. Brands	Established	None
8. Documented assets	More	None
9. Contracts	Comprehensive – done formally	Few – verbal only
10. Industry sector	Market dependent	
	Tech based	Traditional
11. Growth potential	High	Low

All of the factors are important, and almost all of them can be improved upon by the entrepreneur. You can even change your industry sector (eg, moving a traditional retail store online).

Several years ago, I took part in a survey of chartered accountants. We were given three businesses to value. The X (future profits) was the same across all three businesses, but the degree of systematisation was fundamentally different. The Y multiplier was increased on average fourfold simply by the recording, documenting and testing of systems already in place.

What's the point of a balance sheet, then?

Company law defines what a balance sheet is and how it should be put together. The balance sheet governs how much a company can pay out to shareholders in dividends. This is a far cry from telling you how much the business is worth.

The balance sheet commonly doesn't include the full value of 'intangibles'. Why not? Accountants are trained to measure the tangible assets, ie things that have been purchased that last for more than a few years, such as cars, machinery and furniture. They don't measure the intangible assets unless they have been acquired as part of a business purchase. Indeed, international accounting policies require goodwill (the difference between the value of the business and its separable individual net assets) to be written off and effectively removed from business balance sheets.

The intangibles

Many academic studies attempt to explain scientifically what the intangibles are, but the business valuation components diagram below provides an easier way to think of the concept.

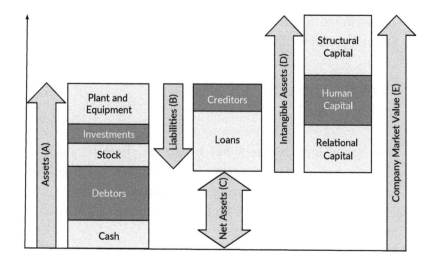

On the left are the 'traditional' assets (A), which, in order of liquidity, are cash, debtors (customer balances owed to the business), stocks, investments, and plant/equipment – all things that have been bought and can be measured with certainty.

Then you have the business' liabilities (B), which are the amounts owed at any given time – overdrafts, loans, amounts due to suppliers, amounts due to the tax authorities, etc.

The sum of (A) and (B) is the business' net assets (C). This number is usually positive. (C) is the figure at the bottom of a balance sheet. But this is where the balance sheet stops. Balance sheets don't take into account intangible assets (D). Often there is more hidden value in (D) than in (A).

The intangibles fall into three main categories.

1. **Human capital** – This comprises your people and
   the subcontractors that work for you or with you.
   You could look at it as the capital that leaves the
   business each night when the doors close. What's
   critical to understand is that human capital cannot
   be owned. Ultimately, your people can give you
   notice and leave. The value of human capital is
   dependent on the abilities and qualities of people
   that make them productive. Some say knowledge is
   the most important factor, but there are many other
   factors, including, but not limited to, motivation,
   ability to change, punctuality and health.

2. **Structural capital** – This is all the intangible assets
   that remain in the business once the human
   capital has left each night. It includes systems,
   processes, procedures, software, technology,
   trademarks, intellectual property, brands, and
   all of the explicit knowledge tools you use to
   produce value for customers.

3. **Relational capital** – This is made up of the
   business' relationships, including those with
   customers, suppliers, network partners, referrers
   and joint venture arrangements. Reputation also
   falls under relational capital.

It's important to understand why these elements are
valuable and important. It all comes down to their effect
on future value creation. The more defined the intangible assets become, the higher their valuation (because

they will have greater income-creation effectiveness). Essentially, the more defined assets you have, the greater the income- and value-generating ability you have.

It's crucial that these assets are not lost when the entrepreneur sells and leaves the business.

In today's knowledge economy, emphasis has shifted away from traditional assets and toward intangibles. Tangibles can be easily bought and sold. Intangibles are much more likely to be unique to your business and can therefore be leveraged to create a premium.

Let's use Nike as an example again. A pair of Nike trainers could retail for around £100, whereas the equivalent unbranded pair would be around £20. In 2017, Nike's worldwide brand value was $29.6 billion.[5] That should give you an idea of the importance of structural capital.

All successful entrepreneurial companies are likely have an abundance of intellectual capital – a subdivision of structural capital, but – and it's a significant but – many are probably not recording and defining it. If it's in your head, it isn't an asset. It must be defined, documented and transferable.

If you want to increase your value, start documenting what the business does, the systems and processes – how it creates value.

---

5   www.statista.com/statistics/632210/nike-brand-value

Where do you start?

To build value, start with the core business.

The goal is to increase structural and relational capital through systems, procedures and contracts, and to be less reliant on human capital, which can ultimately walk away.

The initial task is to map out all areas of your business process, from generating enquiries to collecting income. Then, decide if another person could step in and take over the running of each area. This is what you need to make possible. The process would then be independent of any individual, and you could grow it by adding extra channels. This sounds easy, but in practice you need to work with someone experienced in this field (ideally outside the business) to help you identify each area.

As you create the map, you may be surprised by how many improvements you can make. Once you begin to work *on* the business rather than *in* the business, you will start taking control and building value. You can extricate yourself from the core tasks and work with the intellectual assets.

Below is a basic checklist of the things you need to do to justify and demonstrate value. Once all the tasks have been completed, documented and summarised in a short memorandum, you should be in a position to explain to potential investors and valuers the true worth of your business.

Valuation checklist

Task	Completed
Shareholder/partnership agreements signed	☐
Organisation defined – what is actually included/excluded in the valuation	☐
Marketing systems established and documented	☐
Operational systems established and documented	☐
Patents obtained	☐
Trademarks, designs and copyrights obtained	☐
Values and philosophy defined	☐
Branding document created	☐
Contractual agreements for all relationships signed	☐
• Customers	☐
• Suppliers	☐
• Referrers	☐
• Joint ventures	☐
Three years of independent statutory financial information	☐
Adjusted forecast earnings	☐

Completing these tasks will also increase (Y) in the initial business value equation and, as a result, the business valuation.

People only pay for the value that they can visualise. A written summary of the above will help prospective investors and buyers see the value of your business. Don't just describe something verbally, without any tangible documentary support – prepare a tangible, visible, professionally presented document. You will have much more success.

Independent valuers

It's common for unlisted companies to engage an independent valuer, especially when a shareholder wants to sell or a shareholder dies (the rules around this will be governed by your shareholder agreement, but a valuation will be required). An independent valuer will use expertise and judgement to determine the most appropriate method of valuation.

For a part sale of a business, as a general rule, the valuer will seek to derive a value for the whole business or company. A value will then be attributed to the specific interest. The actual method used to assess whole-entity value depends on the nature of the business and the information available.

A partnership or shareholder agreement, if one exists, may outline a specific method or formula to be used in the valuation process. For companies, in the absence of a shareholder agreement, the articles of association may determine the issue. For partnerships with no partnership agreement, the Partnership Act 1890 is likely to prevail.

It must be recognised that a valuation exercise refers to a theoretical transaction between a hypothetical buyer and seller. It is impossible, in such an exercise, to reflect any premium that might be paid by a special interest purchaser (such as a buyer that is buying your customers to sell both your products and their products) or by a connected party (spouse to spouse); the price such a purchaser is willing to pay will be influenced as much by their own circumstances as those of your business.

In the case of company valuation, the value of an individual shareholding may depend on whether the size of the shareholding warrants any discounts to reflect lack of control (and the reduced attractiveness that would result from a lack of control) or whether the shares should simply be valued on a pro-rata basis. A 25% (minority) share of a business will be less per share than a 75% (majority) shareholding, because the purchaser will have a lot less control.

The value checklist

At the end of this chapter you should understand:

- The foundations on which entrepreneurial business valuations are calculated

- Why balance sheets don't necessarily give the correct answer

- The importance of reducing future risk

- The importance of planning early

- The importance of developing and documenting systems

- Why you should have a checklist of the key areas to focus on to enhance your business value

NINE

Create An Exit Plan

Why, how and when?
Why

At the outset, it's important to understand your motivation for selling the business. This way, a deal that achieves your objectives can be constructed.

There are many reasons for selling, but they typically fall into the following categories.

- **Life goals change:** After many years driving the business forward, the entrepreneur may be seeking a different challenge. They may have a life-changing experience, or for whatever reason, they are seeking a new goal in life.

- **It's no longer fun:** Entrepreneurs are business builders; they are creative, full of ideas and energy. At the start, they probably have great fun running their business. But as the business develops, they might find themselves weighed down by administrative issues. The fun goes out of the business, and selling is the most logical way out (usually to start another business).

- **The business becomes all consuming:** For many entrepreneurs, the business takes over their life. Their personal life can suffer. Selling the business will release funds and time to spend with family and friends, or to pursue other activities.

- **Fresh energy is needed:** The entrepreneur has created a great business, but it has plateaued. It needs an injection of fresh ideas and energy to take it to the next level. At this point, both the shareholders and the company will probably benefit from a sale.

No matter what the reason (and there are many more), it's important to clarify it. Let's move on to the how.

How

Most business owners have lots of experience selling their services or products but very little, if any, experience selling a business. Because it involves large numbers, owners tend to think it's an accounting issue.

The reality is that it's a sales and marketing issue – but this time, it's the business that's the product.

Because business valuation is so entrenched in accounting principles, it's easy to undersell a business. When you sell a product, you sell it based on its advantages to the customer and the value that it delivers. Selling a business is no different. You need to find acquirers that will value the purchase. It's crucial to find out the acquirer's motives for purchasing.

Most buyers buy for future growth; they are looking to expand their existing business. Breaking down the growth motive results in three key areas:

1. **Diversification** – The buyer wants access to your products and services, which have taken years to hone (eg, Google buying YouTube)

2. **Client acquisition** – The buyer doesn't want to spend the time and money growing organically in a new market (eg, Old Mutual buying Skandia)

3. **Geographic expansion** – The buyer wants to obtain a foothold in a new territory (Tata Steel (India) buying British Steel)

Other motives for buying include the following:

- Seasonal balancing (I worked with a business that sold greeting cards in the autumn and winter and plant seeds in the spring and summer)

- Operational and financial synergies (cost savings in the combined resultant business)

- Intellectual property purchase – perhaps the buyer wants hard-to-obtain trade licences in a particular area

- A niche-skilled workforce

- Taking out a competitor

If the main motive is growth, why place a limiting value on a business by taking a historical, formulaic approach? The past can't be changed or recreated. People buy the future and what it can do for them.

If you're negotiating, it's important to maintain the ability to walk away. The best way to do that and still sell your company is to have a range of buyers. You need to keep the buyer in a competitive frame of mind and the balance of control with you, the seller of the business.

I have seen a number of deals where the vendor narrows their options down to one preferred bidder. Once this happens, the bidder has the control. It's amazing how a seemingly wonderful preferred buyer can pull a Jekyll and Hyde change and start reducing their offer as a result of any minor issue. Since the vendor has rejected the other bidders, they're much more willing to accept reductions rather than start the whole process off again.

Put yourself in the buyer's shoes. Imagine you're buying a house. You've just found your dream home, and the seller says there are five people interested. How would you feel? Then, the seller says, 'There is no guide price. Make me an offer.' The seller is in control. You, as the buyer, aren't going to mess about with ridiculous offers.

If you stay in control, you will obtain a better price, the speed of the deal will be greatly accelerated, and the terms of the deal will likely be much more favourable to you.

Along with understanding the buyer's motives, you need to be able to 'sell the future'. The key is to create a vision of what this business will look like in three years under new ownership. Create a different vision for each shortlisted bidder, based on their motives.

Include the following in the vision:

1. The effect on your business of the new owner bringing their clients to buy your products and services (eg, when you sell to a business that has complimentary customers)

2. The effect on the business if the new owner can bring new investment to the existing business (eg, new buyer upgrades your equipment to improve efficiency)

3. The effect on the business with fresh energy, ideas and enthusiasm from a fresh management team, with more relevant experience

4. The effect on the new business taking into account projected synergies and cost savings (common when a competitor buys the opposition and removes duplicate teams)

When you sell the business, don't sell what it looked like under your ownership, past or present. And don't sell what it would look like under your leadership in the next few years – you won't be there!

Take into account the acquirer's management skills and resources to predict future growth. If your buyer isn't prepared to see value in future growth, somebody else probably will. Your sale is providing the foundation for the future growth; neither party can do this alone, so it's reasonable for you both to benefit from the future growth. As a rule of thumb, multiples (Y) range from 1 to 10 for SME private companies.

Investors have access to the same data, so will be unlikely to pay more than seven times future earnings. Buyers will pay above the industry average only if they are strategic purchasers and the vendor keeps control of the deal.

Remember, the value of a business isn't just about the multiple of earnings. If it were, a spread of four to twenty-four would not occur.

Strategic buying

The highest multiple of earnings (Y) I have been involved with is twenty-nine, which involved the strategic acquisition of a UK company by an overseas buyer. The buyer gained access to all the company's blue chip-clients, UK-university clients and public-sector clients.

To achieve a premium price, you need to position your business strategically. Look for buyers that see your business as complementary to their own, not as competition.

The importance of planning and preparation

For some entrepreneurs, selling their business could be the largest transaction they ever undertake. Equally, it could be the first (and only) time they undertake such a deal. Planning and preparation is therefore vital.

What do you need to prepare?

First, compile detailed information on the following:

- Your personal objectives in regards to the sale
- Your ideal purchaser

- The company's:

  - History

  - Differentiators

  - Strengths and weaknesses

  - Finances (last three years, minimum)

  - Staffing

  - Products and services (including how they provide value to customers)

  - Sales and marketing (what you're currently doing)

  - Systems, branding, intangible assets

Then, with this information, create a short prospectus. Why short? Many businesses create lengthy sales memoranda that are far too detailed and boring – and therefore easily ignored. The goal is to give enough information to entice potential buyers to generate an enquiry and request a meeting.

Think of it like a product brochure. What would interest you? The short prospectus should focus on these things:

- Company activity

- Products/services value to customers

- Competitive advantages

- Shareholding/ownership

- Sales and marketing

- Key staff (including why they are key)

- Potential for growth

- Benefits of acquisition to the buyer

- Brief financial overview

Remember, keep it short to keep the attention of the prospective buyer. This is a sales tool, not a statutory compliance form.

As discussed, nobody buys a company for its past performance. Future potential is what matters, so create a business plan that illustrates the potential of the company – how it could look over the next three years under a new owner. Your plan should include new acquirer investment and new clients from the acquirer (along with your existing products and services). You need to help buyers visualise the future asset.

As more business go online there are specifics that acquirers look for that aren't part of traditional business valuations.

Specialist factors such as the following could be required, depending on the nature of the business:

- How stable is the earning power, eg, is the cost per thousand impressions (number of times the product page is viewed) in this niche on the decline/hard to replace?

- What percentage of traffic comes from search? (And what percentage is potentially at risk from changes to the search engine algorithm?)

- How secure are the search rankings? What is the mix of short- and long-tail key words on which potential customers can search?

- How has traffic been trending for the last year? The last few months?

- Has the site been affected by any Google algorithm changes or manual penalties?

- What is the industry trend (see 'Google trends')?

- Where does the referral traffic come from? Is it sustainable?[6]

This isn't a comprehensive list, but it does highlight some of the more recent measures you need to be concerned with when building your business.

Finally, it's also important to remove any nasty surprises. Is there anything in the company's history that potential buyers should know about? Even minor issues that are not disclosed could kill a deal! It's all about building trust.

6 https://feinternational.com/blog/how-do-you-value-an-online-business

You should disclose the following:

- Unresolved litigation
- Tax planning disputes
- Product warranty concerns
- Employee disputes
- Any other similar issues

All of the above is preparation to assist the buyer, but you should also think about your own objectives. What do you want to achieve?

- When would you like to complete the sale?
- What are your views on securing the future for key staff?
- Do you have a minimum price?
- Are you prepared to work with the acquirer for a period of transition?

Exiting a business might seem straightforward, but as this chapter shows, there can be many challenges. You can of course go it alone, but, as highlighted throughout the book, hiring a specialist will likely prove to be a great investment. There are several mergers and acquisitions specialists in the market. As more business go online there are specifics that acquirers look for relating to online businesses that aren't part of traditional business valuations.

Conclusion

Hopefully this book has given you the ability to create and grow a successful entrepreneurial business and to take shortcuts that you might not have considered. I have attempted to keep it simple, with reference to academia where relevant. Research groups are constantly testing new theories of business, but this book is soundly based on practical experience in real situations.

Here's a quick recap to take you through the stages of building a successful business.

Your situation

You are where you are, that has to be your starting point. I have met many business owners in various states of maturity. Very few have reached their potential or are satisfied with their lot. But entrepreneurship is not for everyone. As in any other field, it helps to have some natural talent. That's why I recommend some simple self-analysis to see whether you have the right kind of personality.

Then think about what value you have to offer and whether that can help you fulfil your own personal goals. Does it all make sense both from a monetary perspective and in terms of your life goals?

If starting a business is for you, then begin by setting yourself some realistic targets.

Cash flow

We have seen that cash flow and its management are about much more than just looking at the bank balance. Your bank balance is the result of many actions and systems that you implement or don't implement. Longer-term funding has many options, and careful consideration can reduce risk, tax and give you options to help raise finance with tax breaks for your investors.

Often the entrepreneur just wants to put their idea into practice and doesn't plan until it's too late, but the structure you choose for your business and the intricacies of how it is set up can also have a significant bearing on raising finance and protecting your assets in the event of disputes at a later stage.

HMRC, taxes and red tape

You shouldn't really be running a business if you haven't given yourself a brief education in the regulations and taxation policy that govern what you do.

The rules are there to help all businesses, and many are set with trade in mind. Tax is a bit different: it's there both to raise money for the government and to a degree to shape people's behaviour. Understanding why taxes are raised and the latest government focus (eg, clean energy and electric vehicles), can help some decision making.

If the government is offering tax incentives, either for investment in entrepreneurial business, or investment in R&D, and it's appropriate, you should make sure you make government monetary assistance work for you. I have outlined the various UK business taxes, and you should ensure you are at least aware of what is required. If in any doubt, seek suitably qualified professional help.

Identify insights

I am sure readers reading this think I'm stating the obvious. I am. However, what is obvious is often so obvious that it's overlooked. So many entrepreneurs go on gut feeling and don't really analyse the numbers. You can do good deals that could be better; you can think things are going well, but could they be improved? A classic problem is chasing sales at any cost. High sales may look great, but if they are at low margin, you may simply be running faster on a treadmill that is speeding up.

Set up your own business blueprint, of what matters to you and start monitoring how it's all coming together. Such insights allow you to make decisions, spot trends, identify problems, fill gaps and generally give you the information you need to take your business to the next level.

Enhance the business

We have seen that the pace of business change accelerates every year. Communications, technology and social media all make change faster. Apple's value increased at an average rate of $35.8bn per year over the past 20 years. Better to be on that list than on the list of businesses that were too slow to adapt, like Yellow Pages.

You need to focus on what your value to your customers is, then focus on the key growth factors. Package whatever you do in a way that is congruent with your values. Make sure your price is right – remember, a 1% price change can increase your profits by 10%. Use human nature to ensure you tap into customers' buying psychology, to maximise the value you give to your customers. Systematise what you do to enhance the buyers' experience. Remember productisation and use it to your advantage. Remember to think of your people and take them on the journey with you.

Build value

Think about building value throughout your journey. Business value is based on future profitability *and* low risk. To maximise business value you need to maximise the future profit growth and minimise future risk. All business valuations have a degree of subjectivity, because nothing is certain in the future.

You need to register all your intellectual property, so that it's definitively yours. You can't sell what you don't own. Equally, you can't protect it from the competition if it's not yours. I outlined the importance of documentation and systems testing to help you maximise the value of what you own.

Create an exit plan

Possibly the most forgotten area of business is the the exit strategy. I have outlined the key reasons for selling, and the key reasons for acquirers buying a business. You need to shift your mindset to think of your business as if it's a product: create a brochure for your business, highlight its benefits for its customers and, most importantly, its benefits for your potential acquirers. Keep more than one interested acquirer until that deal is done.

Over to you

Thank you for taking the time to read this far. But to gain the most benefit from the book you need to take action. To help you take the next step into implementation. I have developed a few resources at www. achieveyourbusinessvision.co.uk.

- Take our DISC assessment to find out if entrepreneurship is really for you

- Join my blog, where new ideas related to sections of the book will be discussed regularly

- Book a 'pre-flight' discovery session

- Book a 'pre-flight' seminar

- Enrol on our ACHIEVE programme

Acknowledgements

Several years ago, I had an idea to write a book to help entrepreneurs. As you will have noticed in the text, entrepreneurs need support to create the world we all want to live in. At the time, few people around me believed I could make it happen. However, self-belief can overcome adversity, and with the help of Rethink Press, the outline started to take shape.

Then it took focused effort and time, and that required the support of all the team at Pentins Business Advisers, who allowed me the time to dedicate to this book.

No two days of my working life have been the same – or even remotely similar – since I started working with entrepreneurs. Without all the clients I have worked with over the years I wouldn't have had anything to write about, and would have had a much less stimulating business life. They deserve much credit for following their entrepreneurial aspirations.

The book might never have been completed without the valuable review insights from Steve Lockyer and Derek Mason, who both helped to focus my thoughts in the correct direction.

Finally, my family have put up with my highs and lows throughout the drafting of this text – it's taken so long my children are both adults now!

The Author

Alan grew up in the north east of England and he has personal experience of the decline and fall of industrial Britain in the late 1970s, and of the devastating effect on families and society.

He read for a degree in Physics and Electronic Systems at Brunel University while working at British Aerospace plc. He then trained and qualified as a Chartered Accountant in Cambridge.

Having worked for large and small businesses, he believes very strongly that small business entrepreneurs are the lifeblood of modern society. He has spent over thirty years helping businesses grow, and over the period has seen many ideas that have worked and many that have failed.

But every true entrepreneur has the potential to create wealth and hope both for themselves, their team and the families around them, and Alan is passionate about helping entrepreneurs succeed.

When not working with entrepreneurs he spends time organising county swimming events, including several at the 2012 Olympic venue, to help young people maintain a focus during their teenage years.

Contact details

Website: www.achieveyourbusinessvision.co.uk
Email: adavidson@pentins.co.uk
Telephone: 01227 763400
Mobile: 07798 950414